BUDAPEST

in your pocket

MICHELIN

Travel Publications

MAIN CONTRIBUTOR: LOUIS JAMES

PHOTOGRAPH CREDITS
All photos supplied by The Travel Library
A Amsel 86, 95, 97; Stuart Black front cover, back cover,
title page, 10, 12, 15, 16, 18, 21, 23, 25, 26, 28, 29, 31,
33, 35, 36, 39, 40, 42, 45, 48, 50, 51, 53, 54-55, 59, 61,
62, 63 (right), 65, 66, 68, 70, 71, 73, 75, 76, 77, 79 (top,
bottom), 81, 82, 83, 89, 91, 92, 102, 104, 105, 113, 116,
119, 122; Peter Cox 108, 124; Sue Cunningham 5, 6, 9,
27, 30, 46, 56, 58, 63 (left), 69, 80, 84, 88, 93, 98, 100,
103, 107, 110, 115, Greg Evans 47.

*Front cover: View across the Danube to Parliament; back cover:
boating in City Woodland Park; title page: Fortuna utca*

MANUFACTURE FRANÇAISE DES PNEUMATIQUES MICHELIN
Place des Carmes-Déchaux – 63000 Clermont-Ferrand (France)
© Michelin et Cie. Propriétaires-Éditeurs 1997
Dépôt légal Mai 97 – ISBN 2-06-651601-5 – ISSN 1272-1689
No part of this publication may be reproduced in any form
without the prior permission of the publisher.
Printed in Spain 01-01/3

MICHELIN TRAVEL PUBLICATIONS
Michelin Tyre plc
The Edward Hyde Building
38 Clarendon Road
WATFORD Herts WD1 1SX - UK
☎ (01923) 415000
www.michelin-travel.com

MICHELIN TRAVEL PUBLICATIONS
Michelin North America
One Parkway South
GREENVILLE, SC 29615
☎ 1-800 423-0485
www.michelin-travel.com

CONTENTS

INTRODUCTION

It has been said that Budapest is built on water, and is known as 'Queen of the Danube' for its many spas. The 'dustless highway', as medieval chroniclers called the Danube flowing between Buda and Pest, was once a frontier line for the Romans, then a trade and invasion route for others. On each side of it, hot water trapped by a geological fault gushes to the surface, producing a myriad of exploitable springs. Small wonder that the original Celtic inhabitants called their settlement on the Buda bank 'abundant waters', a name adapted by the Romans to Aquincum.

The three cities of Budapest (Buda, Pest and Óbuda) have been fought over time and time again. Since Béla IV built the first stone fortress on Buda Hill after devastation by Mongols in 1241-42, no less than 31 sieges of the fortifications have been plotted by archaeologists. The stoical, not to say pessimistic, attitude of the city's inhabitants is a reflection of this violent and precarious past.

Behind the façade of tourist attractions – the kitsch of csárdás, gypsy bands and steaming bowls of goulash – there lies a world of ingenious survivors and talented dreamers. The dreams are reflected in some of the overblown 19C architecture, like the enormous eclectic Parliament on the Pest bank of the Danube, or the patriotic monuments on Heroes' Square. But alongside the chasers of dreams are the shrewd entrepreneurs with their feet firmly on the ground, the men who made Pest into a great hub of business in the 19C.

In the late 20C, as Hungary steps out on

the uncertain road to democracy and free markets after decades of totalitarian Socialism, Budapest has again become a city of contrasts. The grey, uniform patina of 'Communism' has been replaced by extremes of conspicuous consumption and visible poverty. Yet underneath the surface gloom and professional pessimism, the people are showing their resilience. The difficult transition has brought out the old qualities of self-irony and survival wit, expressed in the typical Magyar exclamation: 'If only we could *afford* to live the way we do!' When and if that day arrives, there will be something else to complain about...

The Fishermen's Bastion offers far-reaching views across the Danube to the Parliament and Pest.

BACKGROUND

GEOGRAPHY

The historic settlements of Buda and Pest
face each other across the mighty Danube,
less than half way along its 2 820km (1 750
mile) course from the Black Forest to the
Black Sea. Buda, to the west of the river, is
perched on the narrow limestone plateau of
Castle Hill that rises sharply from the river; to
its south is the even more precipitous Gellért
Hill, and to the north 'Old Buda' (Óbuda),
once a picturesque area of narrow streets
fringed by vineyards, but now disfigured with
concrete apartment blocks.

   East of the Danube, Pest sprawls out
towards the Great Hungarian Plain.
Unfortunately, more recent city development
has largely supplanted an earlier and
extremely elegant neoclassical town.

*The old town of
Buda rises from the
banks of the
Danube on Castle
Hill.*

Attached to the Pest side is Csepel Island, formerly the industrial heart of the city. This long sliver of land stretches 54km (33 miles) to the south, giving way to a more congenially residential environment where Prince Eugene of Savoy's Baroque mansion and park (at Ráckeve) are to be found. The city's other important island is Margaret Island, a leafy oasis lying midstream between the northerly reaches of Buda and Pest.

The traditions of the three cities of Buda, Óbuda and Pest (first united in 1873) are very different, and their distinctive features survive, even if post-war concrete sprawl has sometimes blurred the outline of the past. Buda was dependent on the Hungarian court, and subsequently was an imperial administrative centre, its inhabitants, predominantly craftsmen, merchants and caterers, supplying goods and services. Fishermen and traders inhabited the lively Víziváros (Water Town) below the castle on the Danube shore.

The vines of Óbuda also supplied the court, while its German craftsmen, who settled after the Turkish wars, created an infrastructure of workshops and skills. Up till the 19C, the region was often referred to by its German name of *Altofen*. A number of successful light industries, such as river-boat construction and textiles, were added (the Goldberger textile factory still exists).

By contrast, Pest was the merchants' town *par excellence*, growing into a bustling centre of finance and commerce by the late 19C. Even today, it is Buda that seems to be anchored in the past, while modern office blocks and new hotels have changed the face of Pest.

HISTORY

Early Origins

Evidence of cave-dwellers in Buda indicates that the area has been inhabited from at least the **Neolithic period**, while archaeological finds suggest habitation in Pest dates from around 2 000 BC. In the 4C BC, the **Eraviscans**, of mixed Illyrian and Celtic origin, occupied hilltop settlements, the most important being on Gellért Hill. They were, however, no match for the **Roman** legions, who overran their main fort around 10 BC and went on to establish Aquincum (in the Óbuda region) as the seat of the Roman province of Pannonia Inferior (106 AD).

The Great Migrations

Pressure from the east forced the Romans to abandon the town in the 5C, and for the next 500 years the area fell victim to waves of nomadic invaders from the Asian steppe, including the Huns under the feared and admired **Attila**. According to legend, Attila's brother, variously described as Buda or Bleda, bestowed his name on the town.

The modern history of Hungary begins, however, with the occupation of the Carpathian Basin between 896 and 900 AD by the seven **Magyar tribes**, under **Árpád**. The Magyars were at that time nomadic warriors and herdsmen, the descendants of a Finno-Ugric people that originally lived beyond the Urals. They had moved gradually westwards, until about 500 AD, when they were part of a Khazar-dominated alliance of ten tribes (*Onogur* – the origin of the word 'Hungarian') living near the River Don.

The Árpád Dynasty

After a period of warfare and plunder, the Árpád Dynasty established a Christian feudal state under **King István I** (Stephen) (997-1038). King Stephen (later Saint Stephen) invited Gervase Sagredo (Gellért to the Hungarians) to convert his still largely pagan fellow-countrymen, established bishoprics, and welcomed foreign

The bronze figures of Árpád and the other six Magyar leaders guard the base of the Millennium Monument, in Heroes' Square.

9

merchants and craftsmen. His coronation on Christmas Day in the year 1000, with a crown sent by Pope Sylvester II, symbolically anchored the kingdom in the political and religious culture of Western Europe.

After Stephen's death, the greatest Árpád king was **Béla IV** (1235-1270), who rebuilt the country after the genocidal **Mongol invasions** of 1241-1242, which reduced the population by two thirds. Thereafter, Pest grew in importance, receiving a royal charter from Béla in 1244; the first stone fortress of Buda was completed by 1265.

Monument to the great King Matthias Corvinus, during whose reign Buda underwent an architectural Renaissance.

The Angevin Kings, Sigismund of Luxembourg and Matthias Corvinus

With the extinction of the Árpád Dynasty in 1301 the throne passed to the Angevin kings. Under **Charles Robert** (1308-1342) and his successor, **Louis the Great** (1342-1382),

Hungary's territories reached the Dalmatian coastline and even briefly included Naples. From 1335, Buda profited from the staple right (whereby it had a monopoly of sale for certain vital commodities, and which also facilitated the collection of duty).

Between 1387 and 1437 a new palace was built on the southern spur of Buda Hill by **Sigismund of Luxembourg**, who became Holy Roman Emperor in 1410. During his reign, however, the threat posed by the Ottoman Turks first became apparent; the Turks were kept in check (as it turned out, for 70 years) by the great victory of **János Hunyadi** at Belgrade, after Sigismund's death. Hunyadi's son, who reigned as **Matthias Corvinus** (1458-1490), was to be the last king of native extraction, and under him Hungary enjoyed a golden age of humanism.

Turkish Occupation

The glitter and glory of the reign of Matthias Corvinus proved to be the prelude to disaster. The defeat of the young **King Louis II** by the Turks at Mohács in 1526 sealed the fate of Hungary. By 1541 the Turks had conquered Buda itself and for 150 years Hungary was to be partitioned, with only Transylvania retaining any autonomy.

Under Turkish rule, the dwindling Hungarian population was concentrated in Pest while subject peoples from other areas, particularly the Balkans, flooded into the whole area. In Buda most of the churches (including the Matthias Church, *see* p.29) were converted for the Islamic rite, while mosques, *tekkes* (religious seminaries) and baths were built.

RECRVDESCVNT DIVTINA
INCLYTÆ GENTIS HVNGARÆ
VVLNERA

The equestrian statue of Prince Ferenc Rákóczi II, leader of the War of Independence against the Habsburgs, stands in front of the Parliament.

The Habsburgs

The reconquest of Buda by imperial forces in 1686 left the cities once again in ruins, but the way was open for the **Habsburgs** to enforce their claim to the Hungarian throne and extend their hegemony over the whole country. Resistance was centred in the early 18C on Transylvania under **Prince Ferenc Rákóczi II**, who conducted an ultimately unsuccessful War of Independence between 1703 and 1711. The reign of **Maria Theresa** (1740-1780) saw the first signs of a more enlightened approach to the governance of Hungary, involving judicial and educational reforms.

The Age of Reform (1800-1848) and the Revolution

Reactionary attitudes began to change in the 19C, when liberal-minded nobles such as **István Széchenyi** and **Miklós Wesselényi** launched initiatives for reform and modernisation. The driving force was the Anglophile Széchenyi, who promoted diverse projects, including the Chain Bridge, a National Theatre (built in Pest), and regulation of the Danube. Under the popular **Palatine Joseph**, a commission for the embellishment of Pest was set up (1808), to be followed by a less effective body concerned with the improvement of Buda.

The many advances of the Age of Reform were interrupted by the revolution of 1848, which began with a demonstration in Pest and the distribution of a 'National Song' by the young poet, Sándor Petőfi, on the steps of the National Museum. The Hungarians did well at first under their dynamic leader, **Lajos Kossuth**, but in the end the Austrians regained control with the help of the Russian army.

In 1867, Hungary and the now weakened Habsburg dynasty reached an historic compromise (substantially the work of an Hungarian Liberal politician, **Ferenc Deák**) and the Austro-Hungarian Empire or Dual Monarchy came into being.

The Austro-Hungarian Empire

Between 1867 and the outbreak of the First World War, Budapest (as its three towns became in 1872) developed into a flourishing, and now industrial, metropolis with a dramatic rate of economic and population growth. The latter was fuelled by a large influx of Eastern European Jews, concentrated in the Erzsébetvaros area of Pest (VII District), while the wealthy, assimilated Jewish businessmen lived in nearby Lipótváros.

The most significant event of this period was the celebration in 1896 of 1000 years' occupation of the Carpathian Basin by the Hungarians, a huge national exhibition in the spirit of the times that took place on the Városliget (City Woodland Park). The crowning glory of the age was **Imre Steindl**'s great Parliament (1902), a monument to Hungarians' (as yet unfulfilled) aspirations to democracy.

The Disaster of Trianon

Hungary fought with Austria in the **First World War**, despite the forebodings of her Prime Minister, István Tisza, who had counselled restraint. Her defeat in 1918 and the collapse of the Austro-Hungarian Empire led to the brief period of 'Red Terror' during the Communist rule under Béla Kun, and then the **occupation of Budapest** by plundering Rumanian troops. The situation stabilised with the arrival in Budapest of Admiral **Miklós Horthy**. The catastrophic post-war settlement, the **Treaty of Trianon** in 1920, deprived Hungary of two thirds of its historic territory and one third of its Magyar population.

During the Horthy years of authoritarian rule, Budapest did regain some of its sparkle, and its cultural life regained some of its pre-war flair. However, the reality of life in the capital of a country with 'three million beggars' was less glamorous: there were, for a start, 240 000 refugees from the lost territories.

The **Second World War** was a further

Soldiers lost in the First World War are commemorated on Andrássy út.

catastrophe for Hungary. In 1944, Horthy attempted to make a separate peace, but was forestalled by the Germans, who imposed a puppet regime under a right-wing extremist named **Ferenc Szálasi**. Some 600 000 Jews had already been shipped off to the death camps from the countryside, although Horthy did later issue an order attempting to prevent deportation of the Jews in the Budapest ghetto. As Szálasi's men set about butchering remaining Jews, the Swedish consul, **Raoul Wallenberg**, courageously saved a good number by issuing them with Swedish papers (he was later taken prisoner by the Russians and was either killed by

15

them or died in a camp). The war was lost, but the Germans held out on Buda Hill, the final siege lasting nine weeks. Years of war had completely destroyed Budapest's bridges, the palace and the old town, the rebuilding of which was to last until the 1960s. About half a million Hungarians lost their lives in the conflict.

Communism and the Revolution of 1956

In the aftermath of war, Hungary was at the mercy of her new Soviet oppressors, who called themselves 'liberators'. The 'dictatorship of the proletariat' under the ruthless **Mátyás Rákosi** was only eased after Stalin's death in 1953, when Rákosi began to lose support in the Kremlin. Rapid and forced industrialization, which eventually brought the population of Budapest up to a fifth of the whole country, created huge problems of housing shortage and pollution that are still a millstone round the capital's neck.

Hero of the 1956 Revolution, Imre Nagy.

In 1956, the suppressed longing for freedom burst out in revolution. Most of the intellectuals (many of them former Communist sympathizers) turned against the repression and incompetence of the Communists, as did much of the armed forces and the Party's base among the workers. The new government of **Imre Nagy** promised reform and declared Hungary neutral, but was deposed just 12 days later by Russian troops, who brought **János Kádár** to power.

From Communism to Democracy

From the 1960s, Kádár pursued a policy of providing diversions from domestic discontent by allowing some small-scale private enterprise and more personal freedom. However, since the command economy was the cornerstone of one-party power, 'Socialism' could not be reformed without the whole system collapsing. After years of borrowing from the West to stave off domestic unrest, Communism in Hungary simply imploded in 1989. According to some reports, when Kádár was dismissed in May 1988, he broke down, confessed himself a murderer and asked to be shot.

Since Hungary's second ever totally free elections in 1990, she has experienced the familiar difficulties of transition to free markets, at first under the centre-right Christian-National government of József Antall, then under a Socialist-Liberal coalition led by the former Communist foreign minister, Gyula Horn, and since 1998 under the Young Democracy Party led by Victor Orbán.

On the plus side, a substantial programme of restoration has been undertaken in Buda and Pest. Symbolically important was the removal of Communist symbols from buildings, and the renaming of streets. Good food, nightlife and a wide range of cultural events are now available – albeit at prices few Hungarians can afford. Traffic has been eased by the ring road, and even the city's telephone system, hitherto notoriously inefficient, promises to improve through new investment. Budapest may not yet have regained the title of 'Paris of the East', but it is once more becoming a lively and vivid city.

Musical Traditions

In the late 18C, Budapest musicians (most of them Germans) belonged to a highly regulated guild and played religious works, incidental music for drama, or contemporary operas; Mozart's *The Magic Flute* was first performed in Pest in 1793. A group also played Hungarian music and there were already gypsy ensembles specializing in Hungarian folk dances for balls.

The folk dance (and its concomitant tradition of violin virtuosos) evolved from the 18C *verbunkos*, the music played by gypsy bands accompanying the recruiting militia across the land to introduce a sinister air of festivity into the conscription process. The *csárdás* (dance), that so appeals to tourists today, was to be heard in rustic taverns throughout the land.

Béla Bartók (1881-1945) and **Zoltán Kodály** (1882-1967) went back to the roots of the Hungarian folk music in developing their own modern idiom, which remained faithful to the un-Western scales and irregular rhythms of its inspiration. While Bartók's fame spread round the world, and his exile in America made his name

Magyar folk dancers performing outside Buda Palace.

familiar on Western concert programmes, Kodály remained more of an Hungarian phenomenon. However, the latter's teaching methods made him a celebrity, as did a number of his courageous gestures against Stalinism, whose minions felt it unwise to persecute him openly. Kodály's beautiful *Psalmus Hungaricus* (1923) was written to celebrate the 50th anniversary of the union of Buda with Pest.

Perhaps the most famous Hungarian composer, **Ferenc (Franz) Liszt** (1811-1886) was also inspired by Hungarian folk tunes. In 1823 he gave his first concert in Pest as an 11-year-old virtuoso pianist, and in 1839 he gave another concert for the benefit of the victims of the terrible flood that had overwhelmed Pest the previous year. A passionate Hungarian patriot, Liszt was the founder of the **Academy of Music** (1875), which began its proceedings in three rooms above his apartment. Since then, a stream of illustrious performers have issued from the Academy's doors. They include Antál Doráti, Eugene Ormándy, György Szell and Sir Georg Solti.

Contemporary with Liszt was another Romantic composer and patriot, **Ferenc Erkel** (1810-1893), over whose historical opera *László Hunyadi* Berlioz enthused on his visit to Pest in 1846. Erkel composed the quintessential national opera, *Bánk Bán*, based on a patriotic drama by **József Katona**, which is almost always showing in Budapest but has made little impact elsewhere.

During the period of the Austro-Hungarian Empire, Hungarian composers such as **Ferenc (Franz) Lehár** and **Emmerich Kálmán** turned out enormously popular operettas which were inspired partly by Jacques Offenbach, as well as by local theatrical traditions. Works like *The Merry Widow* and *Land of Smiles* remain favourites, while *The Gypsy Baron* (1885), based on a story by the Hungarian Mór Jókai and with music by Johann Strauss II, was unique in being a genuine 'Austro-Hungarian' cultural product.

Musical traditions are very much alive in Budapest today. Contemporary Hungarian pianists of the stature of Zoltán Kocsis and Dezsö Ránki, composers such as György Ligeti and György Kurtág, and other musicians such as András Schiff or Miklós Perényi, have reminded the world of Hungarian musical genius. Folk music, too, has seen a revival in the hands of the Muzsikás group and the singer, Márta Sebestyén.

MUST SEE

Országház★★★ (Parliament)

Imre Steindl's neo-Gothic building dominates the river bank on the Pest side (GU). It took 20 years to build, has ten inner courtyards and 691 rooms. The highlight of the interior is Mihály Munkácsy's huge panoramic painting of *The Magyar Conquest of the Country*, recalling the entry of the seven Magyar tribes into the Carpathian Basin; and it now houses **St Stephen's Crown★★**, of mystical significance to Hungarians.

Looking across the Chain Bridge and Danube towards the magnificent Parliament.

Hősök tere and Szépművészeti Múzeum★★★ (Heroes' Square and the Museum of Fine Arts)

György Zala's great sculpture of Árpád and the tribal chieftains dominates the square. Behind it is the arcaded pantheon of Hungarian leaders, and to the north, the capital's rich collection of non-Hungarian paintings, graphics and sculpture are housed in the Museum of Fine Arts.

Budavári Palota★★★ (Royal Palace)

The massive Royal Palace, situated on Castle Hill (FV), is home to important cultural facilities and museums, such as the Ludwig Múzeum, the **Budapesti Történeti Múzeum★** and the Széchenyi National Library. The **Magyar Nemzeti Galéria★★** is the nation's repository of Hungarian fine art treasures, containing masterpieces from all periods, together with works by little-known artists.

Széchenyi lánchíd★★ (Chain Bridge)

A Budapest icon, the imposing Chain Bridge (FGV), designed by an Englishman and built

by a Scotsman, links Central Pest with Buda.
Lateral cat-walks tempt you for an evening
stroll.

Magyar Nemzeti Múzeum★★
(Hungarian National Museum)
Mihály Pollack's somewhat dour,
neoclassical museum (HX) presents the
history of Hungary from AD 1000 to 1990.

Iparművészeti Múzeum★★
(Museum of Applied Arts)
One of the remarkable works in Hungarian

21

national style by Ödön Lechner, its Moorish-looking interior hall, with sugar-icing contours and cornices, is an exotic architectural folly (HX). It houses period reconstructions of Hungarian and European interiors, and displays of folk arts and crafts.

Mátyás Templom★★ (Matthias Church)

The 19C successor to Buda's 13C coronation church (substantially altered by Matthias Corvinus) is a much-loved national shrine, a stunning example of neo-Gothic architecture with its impressive varnished tile roof.

Gellért Gyógyfürdő★★★ (Gellért Spa)

The most exotic of Budapest's many spas (GX). The exterior is a bizarre, overblown example of Art Nouveau style, while the sensuous atmosphere of the interior is enhanced by pink columns, ceramics and nine baths, one of them with artificial waves (open summer only).

Magyar Állami Operaház★★
(State Opera House)

The most compelling and graceful work by the prolific Miklós Ybl, this neo-Renaissance masterpiece with its arcaded and balconied façade houses the State Opera (HU), whose musical directors have included Gustav Mahler and Otto Klemperer.

New York Káveház★★ (Café New York)

Also known as the Hungaria Restaurant, the famous writers' café has seen better days, but it is still an experience to sit on the marbled terraces overlooking the restaurant-well and nurse a coffee or a schnapps for an hour or two.

WALKS IN BUDAPEST

BUDAVÁRI PALOTA★★★
(ROYAL PALACE AND MUSEUMS)

Beginning below the Palace at Szarvas tér (Bus 78 from Pest or Bus 86 on the Buda side), this walk takes us through the rebuilt Royal Palace (or Castle Palace) with its three museums and the remains of the former residence of the Hungarian kings. It ends at the Sikló (funicular railway), that descends to the Danube (Clark Ádám tér)(FV).

Before climbing northward to the Palace remnants, a detour to the right brings you to some **Turkish graves** under a locust tree, a legacy of the 145-year Ottoman occupation of Buda. From here, bear left towards the grim **Buzogány-torony** (Mace Tower) and go through the **Ferdinand Gate** beside it, leaving other medieval bastions and the formidable curtain walls running to the Danube on your right. Steps up from the walled palace gardens lead you eventually to the southern entrance of the **Budapesti**

The extensive Royal Palace has its origins in the 13C, but underwent re-building after the Second World War.

Történeti Múzeum★ (Budapest History Museum, Wing E).

On the upper floor of the museum is an exhibition covering the history of Budapest since the reconquest in 1686. A rather sparse display of the medieval period occupies part of the ground floor, but a special room along the corridor from the ticket desk is devoted to the beautiful and atmospherically lit **Gothic statues** from the time of the Emperor Sigismund (1387-1437). These were unearthed during excavations in the Palace grounds in 1974: one group is thought to depict courtiers at the Angevin court, while others, in a different style, may be apostles and prophets.

Returning to the lobby, descend to lower levels for a ramble through the Gothic remnants of Sigismund's so-called 'Friss' (new) Palace and the Renaissance extensions and alterations made by Matthias Corvinus (1458-1490). The latter predominate, since much of the earlier building was destroyed when a Turkish gunpowder store exploded in 1578. The highlights are the **Royal Chapel**, the oldest part of which dates to the Angevin dynasty, and the Gothic Hall. Practical artefacts include kitchen utensils, an ice-pit, and a cistern to which water was pumped from the Danube by a horse-driven device.

Leave the museum by the main (north) exit, which is flanked by statues representing **War** and **Peace**. After walking through the courtyard with the **Széchenyi National Library** on your left, you come to the **Lion Gateway**, whose fearsome guardians were sculpted by János Fadrusz (1904). On the other side of it is Alajos Stróbl's romantic

The bronze statue of the Matthias Fountain shows the young King Matthias hunting.

Matthias Fountain★ (1904). It represents the legend of fair Ilonka, who encountered Matthias Corvinus when he was out hunting one day and lost her heart to this handsome stranger, not knowing he was the king.

Walk east through the archway and onto the terrace, which offers a fine **view**★★ of the Danube and Pest. You share the view with **Prince Eugene of Savoy** on his steed (József Róna, 1900). On the plinth, the Turks Prince Eugene captured are depicted in various attitudes of submission and defeat. Beyond is the entrance to the **Magyar Nemzeti Galéria★★** (Hungarian National Gallery), exclusively devoted to Hungarian art from the Middle Ages to the present, including works from the former historic territories of Hungary. Look out for the **19C history painters** with their vivid scenes from the nation's turbulent past, the *plein air* painters of **Nagybánya** (especially Károly Ferenczy and Béla Iványi Grunwald), and the great Hungarian maverick, **Tivadar Csontváry Kosztka** (1853-1919). Hungarian painters are little known abroad, but one who made an international reputation was **Mihály Munkácsy** (1844-1900), whose full range from genre painting to romantic realism is exhibited here.

The rear entrance to the Hungarian National Gallery.

The raven motif found in the Palace derives from the coat of arms of Matthias Corvinus.

To reach the third museum in the complex, walk back through the archway towards the Matthias Fountain and turn right, passing a sculpture of an **Hungarian ostler**. Wing A holds temporary exhibitions on aspects of life in recent times, examined from a socio-economic or political perspective. The **Ludwig Múzeum** (Ludwig Modern Art Collection) occupies the upper floors and is devoted to modern Hungarian and international art.

As you leave the museum and walk north, you pass through striking wrought iron gates, a modern design with a hint of Art Nouveau, which incorporates the raven motif of the coat of arms of Matthias Corvinus. A stroll eastwards across St György tér brings you to an attractive **neo-Baroque gateway** by Gyula Jungfer, beyond the east end of which is the sculptured **Turul**, the legendary bird that sired the Árpád dynasty by mating with Emese. Several such sculptures were made for the millennial celebration of 1896, but only the Buda turul and one overlooking Tatabánya, in Transdanubia, survive. The entrance to the Sikló is north of the gateway.

The Sikló (funicular railway) not only offers an easy way up the steep Castle Hill, but provides wonderful views on the way.

THE OLD TOWN OF BUDA★★

This walk begins with the Sikló (funicular railway), for which the end stop is Clark Ádám ter (FV) (Bus 16 from Pest or 86 along the Buda bank). It covers the sights of the town of Buda on Castle Hill, with its charming streets which have been carefully restored, making this walk a most memorable experience. The walk ends at the Bécsi Kapu (Vienna Gate minibus to Moszkva tér) (EU).

The **Sikló** (open 7.30am-10pm) affords marvellous views over the river and Pest as you rise from Clark Ádám tér to Szent György tér (Castle Hill). It was built in 1870 and was originally operated by steam power; after destruction in World War II, the newly electrified funicular re-opened in 1986.

As you leave the top exit, you will see on your right the neoclassical **Sándor-Palota** (Sándor Palace) formerly the Prime Minister's residence. A plaque on the wall commemorates Count Teleki, the Prime Minister who committed suicide when Hungary joined with Germany in attacking Yugoslavia in 1941. Enter here for the waxworks of Hungarian historical figures.

Walking north, you will pass on your right the **Várszínház** (Castle Theatre) (FV), whose performances were originally in German, the first in Hungarian being in 1790. On your left are the ruins of the **War Ministry**, where rebuilding has at last begun some 50 years after its destruction. Next comes the medieval market area, now called 'Parade Square' (Dísz tér), a military appellation that is underlined by the **Statue of a Hussar** to the south-west and György Zala's **Honvéd memorial** to the north, which recalls the taking of Castle Hill by Hungarian forces during the revolution of 1848. Continue

The western façade of Matthias Church. In front is the Plague Monument, commemorating lives lost in the epidemic of 1691.

into Treasurers' Street (Tárnok utca), passing on your left a Baroque **apothecary's shop** (No 18).

At the end, on the right, is the **Mátyás Templom★★** (Matthias Church) (FU), so-called because the great Renaissance king of Hungary enlarged the earlier Gothic church on this site and was twice married in it. There has been a church here since the reign of Béla IV (1235-1270), but what you now see is Frigyes Schulek's masterly reconstruction (1874-1896), which followed the 13C plan but added some embellishments, notably the spire. The

The interior of Matthias Church is adorned with beautiful frescoes; these depict the lives of the saints.

lustrous interior is painted with polychrome decoration and frescoes by Károly Lotz and Bertalan Székely, the frescoes featuring lives of the saints and Árpád legends. Most notable are Lotz's painting in the **Loreto Chapel**, which shows Pope Calixtus III ordering the bells of Christendom to be rung at midday in perpetuity, to celebrate the great victory by János Hunyadi over the Turks at Belgrade (1456); and the same artist's scenes from the life of St Ladislas (1077-95) in the chapel to the left of the chancel. The stained-glass windows show events in Hungarian history. In **St Stephen's chapel** are scenes from the saint-king's life, the **Royal Oratory** displays Habsburg coronation robes, and there is an exhibition of ecclesiastical treasure in the north gallery.

Flanking the church on the Danube side is the **Halászbástya** (Fishermen's Bastion) (FU),

The seven turrets of the Fishermen's Bastion represent the seven Magyar tribes.

a piece of symbolic architecture built for the 1896 millennium celebration by Schulek, but not completed until 1902. The neo-Romanesque bastion features seven turrets, emblematic of the original seven Magyar tribes.

The appellation is (doubtfully) ascribed to the fact that the Fishermen's Guild defended this part of the castle walls in the Middle Ages. There are fine **views**** over the Danube and to the Parliament from the Fishermen's Bastion. Nearby is Alajos Stróbl's **equestrian statue of Saint-King Stephen I (Szent István)**, who bears an Apostolic Cross in his hand, as converter of his people.

Steps lead down to the Vizíváros (Water Town) from the bastion, but we return to **Szentháromság tér** (Holy Trinity Square), noting the Baroque **Plague Monument** in the centre, actually a reconstruction of P Ungleich's 1714 work, built as a memorial to lives lost in the plague of 1691 (*see* p.29). On the south-west corner of the square is the **Old Town Hall** of Buda (1710). The **Pallas Athene** below the beautiful oriole window bears the arms of the city on her shield.

A detour along Szentháromság utca brings us to the famous **Ruszwurm Café** (No 7), with its fine Biedermeier interior. It was once so esteemed that its pastries were ordered from Vienna, and it still sells the best cream slices in town which will fortify you for more sightseeing.

Four streets run north-south, and parallel to each other, through Buda town. Starting from the westernmost, there are a number of interesting features to note as you walk along them.

Úri utca★★

At No 9 in the southern part of 'Lords Street' (EU) is the **Budavári Labirinthus**, an underground waxwork display of Budapest history concentrating on the bloodcurdling (closed Dec-Jan). Castle Hill is honeycombed with 10km (6 miles) of passageways and chambers where the residents once took shelter in time of siege. Some 80 wells were also dug here to ensure the water supply.

At the junction with Szentháromság utca is the **monument to András Hadik** (1710-1790), who briefly conquered Berlin for

Úri utca, in the Castle Quarter, is where noblemen and wealthy merchants built their residences, and has an attractive variety of architectural styles.

Maria Theresa during the Seven Years' War. A special feature of the northern part of the street are the **Gothic sedilia** and some other Gothic remnants (Nos 32, 34, 36, 38 and 40). At the north end is the ruined **Magdolna Templon** (Church of Mary Magdalene), where Buda's Hungarian community worshipped in medieval times. Under the Turks it was shared between Catholics and Protestants until 1605, when this, the last Christian church to operate, suffered the same fate as the others and was turned into a mosque.

West of Úri utca, the **Tóth Árpád sétány★** is a promenade on the rampart overlooking the Christina suburb with views of the Buda Hills. The southern end of Úri utca runs into **Kapisztrán tér**, with a monument to the Franciscan preacher, **Capistran**, who fought with the Hungarians against the Turks. In the north-west of the square is the **Hadtörténeti Múzeum★** (Museum of Military History) (EU), which traces the military history of Hungary from the 16C. On the northern Angevin bastion is a modern **monument to the last Turkish pasha**, killed in the 1686 reconquest of Buda.

Országház utca

Retrace your steps southwards along Országház utca (Parliament Street), so-called because the former convent of St Clares (No 28) was used for the **Hungarian Diet** in the 18C. It also housed the Supreme Court for a while, and now belongs to the Hungarian Academy of Sciences, which allows periodic concerts in the Great Hall. The street was the Italian quarter in the Middle Ages and Gothic features can still be seen on some houses (Nos 18-22).

Wander along the streets of the Castle area and take a stroll through Buda's history.

Fortuna utca★★

Parallel to Országház utca is Fortuna utca
(EFU 36) which has many Baroque town
houses. Nearly opposite the Hilton Hotel
(*see* p.36) is the **Fortuna Passage at Hess
András tér 4**, leading to a charming
courtyard containing the **Litea Bookshop**.
You can drink exotic herbal teas or coffee
while browsing through a wide selection of
books in English and other languages. Other
shops sell articles of folklore and there is a
terraced restaurant.

The house at No 4 was the printery of
András Hess, who produced here Buda's
first printed work, the *Chronica Hungarium*
(1473). On the same square is József Dámkó's
monument to Pope Innocent XI (1936), who
rallied the forces of Christendom against the

*Typical houses with
painted façades line
Fortuna utca,
leading up to
Matthias Church.*

Turks in 1686. Note also the **House of the Red Hedgehog**, with its hedgehog wall sign, occupying the site of an ancient tavern.

Also in Fortuna utca is the **Kereskedelmi és Vendéglátóipari Múzeum** (Museum of Commerce and Catering), housed in the former Fortuna Inn which gave the street its name. This is a nostalgic place with old posters in the commerce section and traditional tools of the confectioners' trade on show in the catering part.

Táncsics Mihály utca★★
The eastern parallel street (EFU 150) runs from Béla Pinter's **Hilton Hotel**, a modern building integrated into the former Dominican church and monastery. It

Vienna Gate Square has some attractive 18C and 19C houses; at its centre is a fountain with a statue of a woman holding a lamp, in memory of Ferenc Kazinczy.

incorporates the Church of St Nicholas, on the tower of which may be seen a **relief representation of Matthias Corvinus**, a copy of a 15C original, and considered to be the only authentic likeness of the great Renaissance king that has survived.

At No 7 is the Baroque **Erdődy Palace** (1769) by Matthias Nepauer, which is now the **MTA Zenetörténeti Múzeum** (Institute of Musicology) and contains the **Béla Bartók archive**. Its collection of musical instruments is well worth visiting. Here and in the Dominican court of the Hilton, open air summer concerts are held.

Further along the street is the **medieval Jewish quarter**, with a small museum at No 26. A wall chart shows the location of Buda's Jewish community through the ages, until its eradication by the Christian armies that reconquered Buda in 1686.

On **Bécsi kapu tér** (Vienna Gate Square) (EU) are the ungainly **state archives** to the south, opposite the rather plain **Lutheran Church** and a memorial to **Ferenc Kazinczy**, the moving spirit behind the revival of the Hungarian language in the late 18C. Béla Ohmann's 1936 **monument to the recapture of Buda** in 1686 stands in front of the **gate**★ and takes the form of an angel holding a cross. Just outside the gate, below and to the right, is the **Európaliget** (Europe Park) a plantation of trees dating from 1973, when mayors from around the world were invited to plant a tree in commemoration of the 100th anniversary of the union of Buda, Pest and Óbuda. To the left of the gate is Imre Varga's statue of the independence hero and land reformer, **Mihály Táncsics**. The minibus (*várbusz)* for **Moszkva tér** (buses, metro) stops just before the Vienna Gate.

GELLÉRT HILL✶✶ – THE WATER TOWN✶ – HILL OF ROSES

This is a long walk and involves some steep slopes. It is always possible to take Tram 19 from Szent Gellért tér along the waterfront, direction Batthyány tér, stopping at places of interest. Thereafter take Bus 86, direction Óbuda, alighting at Bem tér or Margit-híd.

Gellérthegy✶✶ (Gellért Hill) (FGX), some 235m (770ft) high, can be climbed by the stairway or one of the several paths. The hill is named after **Bishop Gellért**, who was reputedly martyred here in 1046, and is remembered by an imposing bronze statue. There are magnificent **views✶✶** from this point. The **Citadella** (fortress, reached by Bus 27 from Móricz Zsigmond tér, to which run Trams 47 and 49 from Pest) was built by the Habsburgs to keep the Budapestians in order after the 1848 revolution, but never saw action. It houses a restaurant and cheap hotel. To the south is the **Freedom Monument** (1947), now denuded of its statues of heroic Russian soldiers, but retaining Kisfaludy Stróbl's monumental female figure holding aloft a palm of peace. The **view✶✶** from the top is superb, especially at night, and is worth the climb.

The steep descent southwards to the **Gellért Gyógyfürdő✶✶✶** (Gellért spa), housed in the **Gellért Hotel and Thermal Baths**, is through the pleasant **Jubileumi Park** (Jubilee Park). At the bottom of the hill is the reopened **Sziklakápolna** (Rock Chapel), dedicated in 1926, then closed by the Communists who were rumoured to have a bunker inside the hill, but now restored to religious use and cared for by the Hungarian Paulite Order. Across the road is

Set high up on Gellért Hill is the Gellért Monument, the work of G Jankovits (1904); this vantage point offers stunning views of the city.

The indoor baths at the Gellért Hotel offer relaxation in luxurious surroundings.

the Gellért Hotel (GX), whose famous artificial wave **bath★★★** also dates from 1926, although the opulent Art Nouveau hotel and internal baths were completed in 1918, bankrupting all concerned. After a financial rescue, the hotel became a playground for the rich and famous in the inter-war period, when Budapest's most famous chef, Károly Gundel, was responsible for the cuisine.

Whether the setting is Ottoman or Baroque, sumptuous or simply strange, a trip to the Turkish baths is an unforgettable experience!

Another historic spa is just to the north along Szent Gellért rakpart. **Rudas Gyógyfürdő★★** (Rudas Baths) at Döbrentei tér 9, was reconstructed by the Turks, who also built the **Rác Gyógyfürdő** (Rác Baths) nearby on Hadnagy utca 8-10. The interiors of Buda's Turkish baths are romantic, with light filtering from the glass squares of the cupolas through the rising steam. Potential users should be aware that this establishment also attracts a gay clientele.

Leaving the Rác Baths on your left, head north across and under the busy interchange at the Buda end of the bridge into the **Tabán** (FVX), once the settlement of Serbian tanners, the only memorial of whom, after the area was bulldozed in the 1930s, is the Baroque parish **Church of St Catherine** on Attila út. You then pass the **Semmelweis Orvostörténeti Múzeum** (Semmelweis Museum of Medical History), at Apród utca 1-3, once headed by Jószef Antall, Hungary's first Prime Minister after the fall of Communism.

The street leads down to Ybl Miklós tér, in the middle of which is the graceful **Ybl Várkert Kiosk**, designed by Miklós Ybl (1814-1891), and originally the water pumping station for the Castle. It is now a beautifully restored casino-restaurant (*see* p.107). Opposite is a **statue of Ybl**, the architect of the Opera, and across the road is his splendid neo-Renaissance folly, the **Várkert Bazar** (Castle Garden Bazaar, 1882). Built to disguise the pumping station, it had a largely decorative function, recalling the architecture of Italy's hanging gardens with a series of steps and terraces, but was also a fashionable tea-dance locale. Now it has fallen into disrepair.

The Chain Bridge is one of Budapest's famous landmarks.

Continuing north from here, you reach Clark Ádám tér at the Buda end of the **Széchenyi Lánchíd**★★ (Chain Bridge) (FV), where the oval **zero kilometre stone** (1975) measures all road distances from Budapest. Both the **Alagút** (road tunnel under Castle Hill) and the Empire-style Chain Bridge were built by a Scotsman, Adam Clark, the bridge's design being by a noted contemporary industrial architect, William Tierney Clark (no relation). It was completed just before the 1848 revolution, but the plan of the Austrian High Command to blow it up fortunately miscarried. Since 1918 it has borne the name of its initiator, Count Széchenyi, who had thought of the idea in 1820 when thwarted in his attempt to cross the swollen winter waters of the Danube to attend his father's funeral.

From Clark Ádám tér you enter the **Víziváros**★ (Water Town) (FU) so-called because the people who lived on this narrow strip between Castle Hill and the Danube traded from the river. As you head along the embankment, you pass the Post-Modern **French Institute** at Fő utca 17, opened in 1992 on the former site of the French Embassy. On Szilágyi Dezső tér is the neo-Gothic **Calvinist Church** (1896), built over a medieval potters' market. Beside it is a statue of the architect, Samu Pecz, depicted as a medieval mason.

The attractive **Batthyány tér** (Batthyány Square) to the north is named after the Prime Minister in 1848, subsequently executed by the Austrians, despite his moderate stance. On the south side is the lovely Baroque **Szent Anna-templom**★ (St Anne's Church). The high altar statues of the Virgin Mary and St Anne are by Károly

Bebó and the cupola fresco is of the Holy
Trinity. A curiosity is the neo-Baroque
ceiling fresco by Pál C Molnár (1938),
depicting scenes from the life of St Anne.
Beneath the adjacent presbytery to the east
is the fashionable **Angelika** coffee house.

On the west side of the square is a huge
market hall, built in the 1890s, and to the
right of it the former **White Horse Inn**, a
Rococo building located close to the
terminus for the Vienna coach, which is
recalled in the Gyorskocsi utca ('Express
Coach Street') to the rear. The southern
side is occupied by a former convent
hospital of the Elisabethan nuns, whose
Baroque church beyond has a richly
decorated interior which can be glimpsed
through the entrance. In front of the
convent is a statue of **Ferenc Kölcsey** (1790-
1838), author of the Hungarian National
Anthem (*Himnusz*).

If you continue along Fő utca to the
north, you will pass the Nagy Imre tér, newly
christened after the Prime Minister of a
momentarily free Hungary in 1956.
Overlooking the north side of the square is
the gloomy **Military Court of Justice**, where
Nagy was 'tried' before being judicially
murdered.

At Fő utca 82-86 (FU) are the **Király
Baths★★**, a Turkish survival with an attractive
neoclassical extension built in 1826. The
name Király (King) has nothing to do with
royalty, but was the Hungarized form of the
baths' 19C German owners, the König
family. Close to the baths is Mátyás
Nepauer's little **Chapel of St Florian** (1760)
belonging to the Uniate Church, a Greek
Orthodox group in communion with Rome.
Note the pulpit's elaborately carved

Víziváros occupies the narrow strip of land alongside the Danube.

bas-relief, *The Sower of Seeds.*

Fő utca opens out into **Bem József tér,** on the southern side of which is the new extension to the Foreign Ministry, a harmonious design (1996). The statue in the square is of the Polish **General Bem** (János Istok, 1934), who fought for the Hungarians against the Habsburgs in 1848. On the 23 October, 1956, a huge anti-Stalinist rally took place here, the first phase of the revolution. Bem was not only a symbol of Hungarian liberty; the participants were demonstrating in sympathy with the concurrent attempts of the Poles to win freedom from the Russian-imposed regime.

If you continue along **Frankel Léo út** northwards, leaving the **Margit-híd** (Margaret Bridge) on your right, you reach a narrow, cobbled street on your left, **Gül Baba utca**. Some way up this, on the left, steps lead up to the **Gül Baba Türbéje** (Tomb of Gül Baba), situated in the

The curved cupolas of the Király Baths are reminders of its Turkish origins.

Setting off to see the sights from a traditional horse-drawn carriage.

fashionable villa area of the **Rózsadomb** (Hill of Roses). This is the only religious building to survive from Turkish times and commemorates a much-respected Dervish sage, who died during the thanksgiving celebration held by the Turks for their conquest of Buda in 1541. Inside the octagonal tomb are some memorabilia of Gül Baba and the Bektash Order of which he was the leader.

Retracing your steps and turning left along Frankel Léo út, you reach on the left a ruined **Turkish gunpowder mill**, driven by the springs until 1884, and on the right, the **Lukács Baths**, a delightfully old-fashioned spa shaded by plane-trees, with a hospital attached. It is a short walk from here back to the bus connections for Buda and Pest at the Margaret Bridge.

ÓBUDA AND MARGIT-SZIGET★★
(MARGARET ISLAND)

This walk is rather long if Óbuda and Margaret Island are covered in one walk. Start at the Roman amphitheatre (Bus 60 or 86 northwards to Nagyszombat utca from Batthyány tér, or take the HÉV railway from the same square to Timár utca and walk a short stretch back to the south on Lajos utca). Margaret Island can either be approached from Flórian tér, as explained below, or covered in a separate excursion (Bus 26 from Western Railway Station, or from Árpád Bridge metro station).

Óbuda

The great 1C **military amphitheatre** of
Aquincum's★ garrison seated up to 15 000
and, according to legend, was subsequently
used as a fortress by the Huns and (almost
certainly) by Kurszán, one of the chieftains
of the conquering Magyar tribes in the 9C.
Gladiatorial shows were staged here and the
extensive drainage system suggests there
were also water contests.

*The pretty cobbled
Fő tér in Óbuda is
surrounded by
Baroque mansions.*

From the amphitheatre strike diagonally
north-east towards the river, keeping to
Lajos utca, which opens onto parkland.
Ahead of you is the graceful **Óbuda
synagogue** (1821), a neoclassical building
that is used today as a TV studio. Just beyond
it is a truly delightful example of Post-
Modern architecture, the **Hotel Aquincum**, a
rhythmic ensemble of dark glass columns on
the outside, and inside an appealing atrium-
like lobby. To the west is the late-Baroque
Óbuda plébániatemplom (Óbuda Parish
Church), fronted by lawns and a chestnut
avenue. The church was founded by the
local Zichy landlords and built by János
Paur; the interior carving by the Italian
Carlo Bebo and his school is notable,
especially the pulpit, with depictions of the
Good Shepherd, Mary Magdalene and
allegories of Faith, Hope and Charity. Note
also the statues of the apostles on the side-
altars. In front of the church are Baroque
sandstone representations of St Florian and
St John of Nepomuk.

Walk north under the rushing traffic of
the Árpád híd to reach Szentlélek tér, which
leads on into the delightful **Fő tér★**. The
square is rich with the atmosphere of the
forgotten world of Óbuda, with its cobbled
streets, 19C lampstands and several fine

restaurants that have courtyards for eating out in summer. In front of you is the **Vasarely Múzeum★** (Vasarely Museum), containing some of the 400 works of the Op artist, Viktor Vasarély, donated to his homeland from his exile in France. Passing a bust of the writer Gyula Krúdy, who assiduously patronised the watering-holes of Óbuda, you reach the entrance to the **Zichy kastély** (Zichy Mansion). Built in 1757 by Henrik Jäger, this Baroque palace now houses a small **museum of local history**, as well as one dedicated to the multi-talented Hungarian propagandist for avant-garde writing and painting, **Lajos Kassák** (1887-1967). Concerts are held in the courtyard in summer.

Substantial ruins of the Roman town of Aquincum can be explored.

Imre Varga's Walkers in the Rain, on Hajógyár utca are an incongruous sight on a sunny day.

On the west side of Fő tér at No 4 is the interesting **Zsigmund Kun Folk Art Collection**. In Hajógyár utca to the north-east is **Imre Varga**'s amusing sculptural group *Walkers in the Rain*. A **museum** dedicated to this leading local sculptor is close by at Laktanya utca 7.

Scattered throughout Óbuda are numerous **Roman ruins**, the most substantial of which are the former civil town of **Aquincum★**, which can be reached with the HÉV railway. Much of the Roman remains

51

have been excavated. These uncovered remains are open to the public, and include the forum, public baths, arcades, market hall, houses and the infrastructure which once supported this Roman city. At the centre is the **Aquincum Museum**, with displays of sculptures and artefacts from the site. Three stops (northbound) from the Árpád híd, under the bridge, are the former military baths and nearby the remains of a temple on the edge of the park to the west.

It is possible to walk to **Margit-sziget** (Margaret Island) by climbing onto the Árpád híd from the Aquincum Hotel side, but you must then brave the noise and traffic fumes. Alternatively, take Tram 1 from Flórián tér to the far side of the bridge and Bus 26 from there to the island.

Margit-sziget** (Margaret Island)

The island may be approached from the southern end by taking Bus 26 from the Nyugati pályaudvar (Western Railway Station).
Once the hunting ground of kings, Margaret Island became a religious retreat from the 12C. It is named after the daughter of King Béla IV (1235-70), who entered a Dominican convent here, possibly in fulfilment of her father's vow to have her brought up as a nun if the invading Tartars left Hungary.

From the 18C the Habsburg Viceroy owned the island, Palatine Joseph building himself a villa here, besides planting vines and many species of tree. It was opened to the public in 1869 and the connecting link with the Margaret Bridge was built in 1900. It is one of Budapest's best-loved recreation areas, free to all since admission charges were abolished in 1945.

The island is not large and a walk round it

takes about an hour. Sights worth seeing
(starting from the Árpád híd end) include
the **Musical Fountain**, actually an electronic
replica of a 19C device that worked by water
pressure. There are two spa hotels nearby, of
which the restored **Danubius Grand Hotel**
(originally built in 1873, designed by Miklós
Ybl) is the most attractive. It boasts an open-
air restaurant with music and good
(expensive) cuisine. Near the **Danubius
Thermal Hotel Helia**, once the haunt of
Soviet trades unionists, is a charming **rock
garden**. Further south is the reconstructed
Premonstratensian **Szent Mihály Templom**
(Chapel of St Michael), with a 15C bell that
was discovered when a tree blew down in a
storm in 1914. Further south is the **open-air**

*Once a religious
retreat, Margaret
Island has pleasant
gardens where
locals and visitors
can retreat from
the bustle of the
city.*

theatre (opera performances in summer) and the ruins of St Margaret's **Dominican Church and Convent**, together with those of the **Franciscan church**. There are two baths: the massive **Palatinus**, which has several pools, including Budapest's biggest, a wave machine and a capacity for 20 000 people; and the sports-oriented **Alfréd Hajós Baths**, named after Hungary's first Olympic gold medallist in swimming, who also designed the whole establishment.

Towards the southern end of Margaret Island is the **monument** marking the 1972

centenary of the union of Pest, Buda and Óbuda, behind which is a **fountain** lit up at night with a myriad of different colours.

Two charming features of the central part of the island are the **Rose Garden** (east of the Palatinus Baths) and the **artists' grove**, an area north of the Dominican ruins consisting of avenues lined with busts of great Hungarian artists, literary figures and performers. Locals come to Margaret Island to enjoy this leafy, tranquil oasis.

You can leave the island via the Margaret Bridge, or take Bus 26 back to Pest.

The large complex of the Palatinus baths, on Margaret Island, offers a pleasant refuge from the hot summer city.

The Danube and its Bridges

In the late 19C, the sunken piles of a Roman bridge were discovered just to the north of today's **Árpád híd** (Árpád Bridge); this structure must have connected the military and civil town of Aquincum with the military outposts in Pest. Between the Roman era and the 19C, however, there was no permanent bridge over the Danube, although several were planned. From the 16C, the inhabitants made do with pontoon bridges, the most sophisticated built by the Turks; this had to be dismantled in winter because of the ice-flows, and also opened twice every 24 hours to let through river traffic In the 18C, a so-called 'flying bridge' operated, consisting of a boat attached to the banks by long ropes, which swung from shore to shore using only its rudder and the power of the current.

The first permanent bridge was built in the 1840s, the famous **Lánchíd** (Chain Bridge) (*see* p.43), subsequently named after its instigator, **Count István Széchenyi**. **Margit híd** (Margaret Bridge) was the second to be built; construction was by a

French company to a design by Ernest Gouin, and it was completed in 1876 at a cost of five million Gulden. The central kink in the bridge, where it approaches Margaret Island, was not a design fault as the café wits thought, but a device to ensure that the two halves of the bridge were exactly vertical to the current of the Danube on each side of the island.

Szabadság híd (Liberty Bridge) (GHX) was Hungarian-designed and originally named after Emperor Franz Joseph. The replica of the silver rivet that the Emperor struck into the Pest abutment at the inauguration during the 1896 millennial celebrations disappeared during the 1956 revolution. The Hungarian coat of arms appears on the central arches, together with a representation of the turul bird.

The **Erzsébet híd** (Elisabeth Bridge) (GX) was named after the popular Empress Elisabeth and was built between 1897 and 1903. Its construction required the demolition of a large swathe of old Pest, including the neoclassical town hall; the Inner City Parish Church (saved at the time only by popular protest) is now crammed close to the eastern end. The original chain bridge fell victim to German sabotage at the end of the Second World War and the modern suspension bridge was built by Pál Sávoly in 1964. All bridges over the Danube were blown up by the Germans to cover their retreat in 1945.

The modern **Árpád Bridge** started life in the 1950s as the **Stalin Bridge**, but the name was prudently changed after 1956. It is a typical product of its time, and has little to recommend it aesthetically. There are, in addition, railway bridges to the north and south and a new crossing has been built for the recently completed ring road.

Liberty Bridge has a span of 331m (1 086ft).

PEST: BELVÁROS (INNER CITY) AND LIPÓTVÁROS (LEOPOLDTOWN)

Together these areas constitute the V District of the city, the heart of Pest. Apart from a couple of detours, the route lies within the Kiskörút (Small Boulevard) Inner Ring, which runs from Margaret Bridge along Szent István körút, Bajcsy-Zsilinszky út, Károly körút, Múzeum körút and Vámház körút. The end stop is Liberty Bridge. If all the detours are taken, this is a long walk. Its two sections could be done separately, or as morning and afternoon programmes.

The University of Economics is housed in the former main customs building for the port of Pest. It still dominates the river bank, next to Liberty Bridge.

Belváros (Inner City)

We begin at the east end of **Szabadság híd** (Liberty Bridge) at **Fővám tér**, to the south of which is the impressive **Közgazdaságtudományi Egyetem** (University of Economics) (HX), originally the customs building for the port of Pest and designed by Miklós Ybl in neo-Renaissance style (1874). If you can negotiate the doorman, it is worth

he restored
entral Market has
lively atmosphere,
ith busy shoppers
nd stall-holders
lying their wares.

getting inside to see the **atrium**, once the great customs hall of a bustling entrepot.

At Nos 1-3 Vám körút is the **Központi Vasarcsarnok**★★ (Central Market, 1896), now beautifully restored. It was the scene of Mrs Thatcher's photo opportunity on her visit to Budapest in 1984. Walk east to **Kálvin tér**, to find József Hofrichter's somewhat clumsily-designed **Reformatus Templom** (Calvinist Church, 1830) (closed more often than not, unfortunately). It was improved by József Hild's additions in 1854 to the entrance portico, and the internal galleries. The only notable decorations of the austere interior are the fine **Romantic sepulchre** of Sarolta

Strachan, the English wife of Count Máno Zichy, and the **stained glass windows** showing distinguished Transylvanian Protestants, which are by the Secessionist artist **Miksa Róth**.

A short detour along Baross utca brings you to the neo-Baroque **Szabó Ervin Library**, named after a leading Budapest Social Democrat (1877-1918) who did much to improve public education facilities. A longer detour on the arterial **Üllői út** brings you to Ödön Lechner's extraordinary **Iparművészeti Múzeum★★** (Museum of Applied Arts, 1896). The sugar-icing tulip pattern of the stucco in the Indian-inspired interior is a sheer joy and the rotating exhibitions (phased by period and style) are invariably stimulating, the furniture being particularly interesting. Upstairs is a permanent display of arts and crafts.

Returning to Kálvin tér, a detour to the left (Kecskeméti utca) past the new Hotel Korona (built on the site of the city's old Kecskemét Gate) brings you to Andreas Mayerhoffer's lovely **Egyetemi Templom** (University Church), generally considered the finest Baroque church in the city. Down Szerb utca, to the left, is the same architect's attractive **Szerb Templom** (Serbian Church). The walk continues from Kálvin tér, however, along **Múzeum körút** to the **Magyar Nemzeti Múzeum★★** (Hungarian National Museum) (HX) on your right (Nos 14-16). It is easily recognised by Mihály Pollack's classical portico and the **statue of the poet János Arany** (Alajos Stróbl, 1893) in the garden. The highlight of the museum was the **coronation regalia★★**, but the majority of this has been transfered to the Parliament. The museum, housed on three floors, has a

Luxuriant ceramic vegetation overrun the roof and Art Nouveau façade of the Museum of Applied Arts.

isplay of the history of Hungary from AD 000 to 1990.

Múzeum körút ends at **Astoria**, an historic otel where members of Hungary's first epublican government congregated in 918, opposite which is the fine Post-Modern **East-West Trade Centre** (1991). To our right is the long shopping street, Rákóczi út, leading to **Blaha Lujza tér** (one top on the red line of the metro from Astoria). Immediately to the left of the quare at Erzsébet körút Nos 9-11 is the amous **New York Café★★**. In preference to olitary scribbling in often dank lodgings, vriters congregated in literary cafés, and the New York was a favourite. Here, writers had

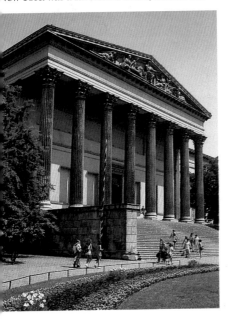

The striking neoclassical façade of the Hungarian National Museum is reminiscent of the Erechtheum on the Acropolis in Athens.

their own specially discounted menu, while paper and ink were provided free, together with foreign newspapers and journals. Try to stop off here for a coffee or a schnapps, and to enjoy the ornate interior, with its heavily gilded columns, walls and ceilings, the frescoes, marble tables and mirrors reflecting the opulent decoration.

Further east is the **Keleti pályaudvar** (Eastern Railway Station), with statues of George Stephenson and James Watt on the façade. To the south in Fiumei út is the **Kerepesi temető** (Kerepesi Cemetery), last resting place of Hungarian heroes (and some recent villains), with interesting tombs.

After this detour, return to the **Kiskörút** on Károly út and you will pass on your right the newly restored **Dohány utca Zainagóga**★★ (Grand Synagogue, 1859) (HV), the world's second largest, and built by the Viennese

The Kerepesi Cemetery contains tombs and memorials honouring many past Hungarian heroes.

architect, Ludwig Förster. The Moorish-looking building is for the 'Neolog' (less strictly orthodox) Jewish community and its precincts house the **Zsidó Múzeum** (National Jewish Museum). In the courtyard at the rear is Imre Varga's moving **weeping willow memorial** to the holocaust (1991) with an inscription translated as '*Whose agony greater than mine?*' This area became a ghetto in 1944 and many Jews perished here from hunger and cold. A good number were rescued by the Swedish consul, Raoul Wallenberg, who provided Swedish papers to extricate them.

Return to the west side of Károly út and turn left down **Gerlóczy utca**, passing the English-language **Merlin Theatre** (also a jazz

The two polygonal towers dominate the entrance to the Grand Synagogue.

Detail of the façade of the Grand Synagogue.

venue) as you go. You exit on **Városház utca**
between the elegant neoclassical **Pest
Megyei Közgyűlés** (Pest County Hall) at No 7
and, to the north, the huge **Városház** (City
Hall). The latter (by Anton Martinelli) was
originally an 18C war veterans' home, but
became the City Hall in 1894. Evening
concerts are sometimes held in the
ceremonial chamber.

Városház utca exits to the north on
Szervita tér (GV 142). To the square's west is
the Baroque **Servite Church** (1732), with a
First World War memorial on the façade. In
the middle of the square is an **Immaculata
column** and at No 3 is the **former Turkish
bank** (1906) with an intriguing Art Nouveau
mosaic in the gable by Miksa Róth. It depicts
Our Lady (as Patroness of Hungary),
surrounded by Magyar heroes.

A left turn down **Petőfi utca** brings you at
the end to **Ferenciek tere** and the striking
Párizsi udvar★ (Paris Arcade, 1911) (HV),
Henrik Schmahl's late Art Nouveau arcade
with a coloured glass cupola. There are
many good restaurants and eating places in
the streets around the square, which is at the
heart of the tourist centre of the inner city.
Across the busy square is the **Ferences
Templom** (Franciscan Church, 1743) with
frescoes by Károly Lotz and a pew where
Franz Liszt used to sit when he lodged in the
Franciscan monastery. A relief on the street-
side wall of the church depicts the disastrous
flood of 1838. The **Nereid Fountain** stands
in the little square in front of the church
and not far to the south is the **Egyetemi
Könyvtár** (University Library, 1876), its
multi-coloured dome handsomely restored
in 1991. Besides over a million books, it
houses rare old manuscripts.

There has been a church on the site of the Belvárosi plébániatemplom (Inner City Parish Church) since the 11C.

Walk towards the **Elisabeth Bridge** (GX) on the north side of Kossuth Lajos utca and you come to the **Belvárosi plébániatemplom★** (Inner City Parish Church) at Március 15 tér, passing by the building of the **Eötvös Loránd University**. It is the oldest church in Pest; the earliest part of the existing church is Romanesque and it has been continuously added to or altered. Its many interesting features include the **Renaissance tabernacles** of red marble and the **Turkish mihrab** (prayer niche) on the south wall.

Just to the north are the remains of the

Roman **Contra Aquincum** camp (GV), and beyond that the **statue of Sándor Petőfi**, the national poet. This has been the focus of 20C political demonstrations in the Second World War, in 1956 and in 1989. We return along **Kigyó utca** to the famous shopping promenade of **Váci utca★**, which is always thronged with people. Post-1989 the trend has been to open fairly up-market shops, mixed with (often down-market) bars and cafés, and other less attractive features of the mass consumer society.

Váci utca is a popular shopping street, with a range of cafés and restaurants.

Váci utca ends to the north in **Vörösmarty tér★**, named after the great 19C dramatist and poet, whose monument dominates the square. Street musicians perform here in summer, but the main feature of the square is the celebrated **Café Gerbeaud★**, the most fashionable in the city, whose pastries are justly praised. It has begun to recover its 19C glamour but cannot quite shake off the tourist trap image. A short walk eastwards brings you to the metro hub at **Deák tér**.

Lipótváros (Leopoldtown)

*All three metros (M1 - yellow, M2 - red, M3 - blue) meet at Deák tér (GV), so it is a good starting place for any walk in Central Pest. In the little street leading off to the south-west from the metro (Sütő utca) is the **Tourinform** office.*

Hard by the metro entrance is the **Evangélikus-templom** (Lutheran Church), mostly the work of Mihály Pollack and completed in 1808. The adjacent **Evangélikus Országos Múzeum** (Lutheran Museum) is particularly interesting in that it documents the enormous contribution Protestants have made to Hungarian life and culture, from Gáspár Károlyi (the translator of the Bible into Hungarian) to leading writers and politicians such as Lajos Kossuth and Bajcsy-Zsilinszky.

Make your way north-west across **Erzsébet tér**, which is now dominated to the south by the lowering **Corvinus Kempinski Hotel**, Budapest's newest and grandest hotel. The **Danubius Fountain** in the square is by Miklós Ybl and represents the Danube itself at the summit, with the three other great rivers of historic Hungary below (Tisza, Dráva, Száva).

An archway to the west brings you into **József nádor tér**, with Johann Halbig's statue

(1858) of the Habsburg **Palatine Joseph** in the centre (*see* p.13). Turn left along **József Attila utca** (GV) at the north end of the square and you soon find yourself on **Roosevelt tér**. This is the area of the three luxury hotels erected in the 1970s and 1980s: the **Regency Hyatt** excepted, they have ruined the aspect of the Pest embankment at its most focal point. Between the **Inter-Continental** and the **Marriott** hotels along the river to the south, is Frigyes Feszl's **Pesti Vigadó★** (Redoubt), built in 1864 in Romantic style but largely reconstructed after wartime damage and

In the Danubius Fountain, by Míklós Ybl, sensuous female figures represent the Danube and its three tributaries.

with a modern interior. It stages an ever-popular programme of Hungarian and Viennese operetta, as well as classical concerts.

Turning back to Roosevelt tér, you will notice in the middle a statue of **Ferenc Deák**, the driving force behind the *Ausgleich* (Compromise) with Austria. At the north end is the **Magyar Tudományos Akadémia** (Hungarian Academy of Sciences) (GU), founded in 1865 on the initiative of Count Széchenyi and built to a neo-Renaissance design by Friedrich Stüler. A relief on the east wall shows Széchenyi offering a year's income for the founding of the Academy. A

The 19C façade of the Pesti Vigadó, a popular entertainment venue.

statue of Széchenyi may also be seen in front of the building. The east side of the square is dominated by a hideous green office building of the 1960s, known (not affectionately) as the **Spinach Palace**. Next to it, however, is the more attractive Art Nouveau **Gresham Palace** (1907), built for a

London insurance company.

Walk north on Akadémia utca as far as **Széchenyi utca**, turn right and walk to **Szabadság tér★** (Liberty or Freedom Square). The eastern side is occupied by the huge state **television studios**, built in an eclectic style by Ignác Alpár (1905), originally as the Stock Exchange. He also designed the **Magyar Nemzeti Bank** (National Bank of Hungary) on the other side of the square. To the south-east of this is József Finta's gigantic **International Bank Centre** (1995). The **obelisk** at the northern end marks the city's liberation by the Red Army.

The **American Embassy** itself is in the Art Nouveau building at the north-east corner of the square, behind which, at Hold utca 4, is Ödön Lechner's famous **Postatakarékpénztár★★** (Post Office Savings Bank, 1900). The design makes colourful use of Zsolnay ceramics, most remarkable in

The obelisk in Liberty Square is Budapest's only Soviet monument still standing in its original position.

The Post Office Savings Bank is one of the city's finest examples of Ödön Lechner's Secession style.

the yellow bee-hives on the roof that symbolise the accumulation of savings. Also look for the various animal and vegetable decorations swarming along the façade.

From here, a short walk north on Hold utca brings you to the **Batthyány Eternal Flame**, an emotive memorial consisting of an ever-burning lamp on a plinth, which commemorates the leader of the Hungarian government in 1848 who was executed by the Habsburgs on this spot.

Head west along Báthory utca, which enters the south-eastern end of **Kossuth Lajos tér** (GU). To your left is the impressive bronze **statue of Imre Nagy**, depicted standing on a bridge over a small pool (*see* p.16). Nagy addressed huge crowds from the Parliament building at the beginning of the 1956 revolution, although his speech (received with disappointment) was meant to calm, rather than excite passions.

Kossuth Lajos tér itself is dominated by Imre Steindl's eclectic **Országház★★★** (Parliament), completed in 1902, the year of Steindl's death. The architect wanted to combine 'medieval style with national and personal features', an accurate description of this monumental edifice of 691 rooms and 20km (12.5 miles) of corridors that was partly inspired by the Houses of Parliament in London. **Tours of the interior** (when Parliament is not sitting) are organised by local travel agents or you can queue at Gate X. There is much to see in one of Budapest's outstanding architectural achievements, the main attraction being **St Stephen's Crown★★**, which was returned to Hungary by the Carter administration in 1978 after being locked up in Fort Knox since the Second World War. It is actually two crowns hammered together, the lower Byzantine, the upper Latin: the 'Latin' one traditionally, but probably erroneously, is identified with that sent to St Stephen by Pope Sylvester II in AD 1000. Other highlights include the domed hall, the ceremonial staircase frescoed by Károly Lotz and the Grand Chamber with Mihály Munkácsy's enormous *The Magyar Conquest of the Carpathian Basin*.

A statue in the park to the east of the Parliament depicts **Lajos Kossuth** calling the people to arms in 1848. To the south of the park is **Ferenc Rákóczi II**, an heroic neo-Baroque celebration of the leader of the War of Independence against the Habsburgs (*see* p.12). Near the river to the south of the Parliament is László Marton's moving representation (1980) of the radical poet **Attila József** (1905-1937), with an inscribed quotation from one of his most famous meditative poems, *By the Danube*. North of

the Parliament is Imre Varga's statue of **Mihály Károly**, the left-wing aristocrat who headed the first Republic of Hungary.

On the east side of the square are two imposing buildings. From the roof of the first, the **Földművelésügyi minisztérium** (Ministry of Agriculture, 1887), Stalinist agents provocateurs shot into the unarmed crowds in 1956. North of it in the **former Supreme Court** (1896) is the **Néprajzi Múzeum★★** (Ethnographical Museum), built by Alajos Hauszmann. The interior is sumptuous, with an impressive staircase and entrance hall. The permanent collection of **folk artefacts** is worth seeing and changing exhibitions display aspects of Hungarian ethnicity and nationhood.

A short walk northwards on **Balassi Bálint utca** brings you to the east end of the Margit híd, from which point buses and trams run.

The monumental Parliament, designed by Imre Steindl, took 20 years to complete.

Szent István Bazilika★ – Andrássy út★★ – Hősök tere – Városliget★

This route may conveniently begin at the metro hub of Deák tér (M1, M2, M3) and involves quite a lot of walking, although you can return to your starting point with the M1 (yellow line) from the Széchenyi gyógyfürdő (Széchenyi Spa) in the Városliget.

As you cross Deák ter to the north-east, you will pass the dramatic statue to the politician **Endre Bajcsy-Zsilinszky**, murdered by the Germans in 1944 when he tried to form a coalition of anti-Nazi forces.

Szent István Bazilika★
(St Stephen's Basilica)

Skirting the modern **trade centre** on the corner of **József Attila utca**, you enter **Bajcsy-Zsilinszky út** and immediately on your left is St Stephen's Basilica (GU), the building of which took 55 years. It was begun by József Hild, but his dome collapsed in 1868, a year after his death, and Miklós Ybl had to start again from scratch. After Ybl's death in 1891, József Kauser completed it (1906). Its architectural eclecticism is of indifferent quality and the inside is so dark that it is hard to appreciate the multitude of statues and pictures. However, it is worth seeking out Gyula Benczúr's *St Stephen Offering the Hungarian Crown to the Virgin Mary* (second altar on the right), a striking example of Historicism; also Alajos Stróbl's **statue of St Stephen** behind the main altar. In the **Szent Jobb kápolna** is the revered relic claimed to be St Stephen's right hand. It is carried in procession through the town on 20 August, the anniversary of Stephen's canonization. You can climb the basilica's dome, for a fine view of Pest.

St Stephen's Basilica is the largest church in Budapest. Neoclassical towers flank the vast portal, built in the form of a triumphal arch; beyond is the dome, the original of which collapsed in 1868.

Andrássy út★★

Retracing your steps on Bajcsy-Zsilinszky út to the major junction with **Andrássy út** (HU), turn left down the latter, the grandest boulevard of the city. Some 2.5km (1.5 miles) long, it was named after a gifted foreign minister of the Austro-Hungarian Empire. (*An alternative way of viewing the sights is to take the yellow Metro [M1] along the boulevard from Deák tér, alighting at any of the six stops up to Hősök tere/Heroes' Square.*)

Andrássy út has some of the finest architecture in Budapest, many buildings

Stained-glass windows depict the Magyar leaders in the Postal Museum building.

displaying individual features such as mosaics, statues or friezes. The first part is flanked by neo-Renaissance apartment blocks designed by Miklós Ybl. At No 5 (on the first floor) is the **Postamúzeum** (Postal Museum) (HV), which documents the history of the service in Hungary. On your left at No 22 you come to the Neo-Renaissance **Magyar Állami Operaház★★** (State Opera, 1884) (HU), the greatest masterwork of Miklós Ybl. It incorporated the most modern safety devices when built, in particular all-metal hydraulic stage machinery (a reaction to the catastrophic fire at Vienna's Ringtheater in 1881). The **façade** is decorated with statues of the great composers, together with figures representing the Muses. The **interior** is lustrous, with a **marbled stairway** frescoed by Bertalán Székely and Mór Than and a ceiling fresco in the auditorium of *Olympus, Home of the Gods* by Károly Lotz. Seven kilograms of gold were used in the gilding and the chandelier requires 260 bulbs!

Opposite the opera, is an early Lechner building which now houses the **Balett Intézet** (Ballet Institute). A detour down the street beside it brings you to the marvellous **Új Színház** (New Theatre) in Paulay Ede utca, a triumphantly reconstructed (1990)

Franz Liszt sits on one side of the entrance to the State Opera; Ferenc Erkel sits on the other.

building in idiosyncratic style by Béla Lajta
(1909). On the façade's parapet, nine gilded
ceramic angels carry the turquoise plaques
bearing the theatre's name. The interior is
even more dazzling, an early incarnation of
Art Deco, with a delightful play of cream
and blue against bowed metal railings,
ubiquitous mirrors and chrome lighting.

Back on Andrássy út, you soon reach on
the right the **Művész cukrászda** café, with its
nicely restored eclectic interior. Crossing the
Nagymező utca, somewhat extravagantly
called the 'Broadway of Budapest' (which it
was until the 1930s), you reach **Liszt Ferenc
tér**, on the corner of which is the excellent
Writers' Bookshop. The latter has a large
selection of books on Hungary in English
and German, a few in French and Italian.
Across the boulevard you will see a statue of
Hungary's most translated novelist, **Mór
Jókai** (1825-1904). Next to you on Liszt tér is
the bronze figure of **Endre Ady** (1867-1919),
Hungary's greatest early modern poet, also
an active cultural and political journalist.

As you walk down the square southwards,
you will see Laszló Marton's wonderfully
dramatic representation (1980) of **Franz Liszt**
giving a virtuoso performance. At the south-
east end is the **Liszt Ferenc Zeneművészeti
Főiskola** (Franz Liszt Music Academy) (FU)
with an idiosyncratic Art Nouveau **interior★**.
Concerts are given in the auditorium, which is
noted for its excellent acoustics.

Returning along the square to Andrássy
út, you continue across the **Oktogon**
junction past the birthplace of the Marxist
philosopher, György Lukács (No 52) and the
former headquarters and prison of the
Communist security services (No 60). At No
67 is the **Liszt Ferenc Emlékmúzeum**, where

Heroes' Square was begun in 1896 as part of the millennial celebrations, and was completed in 1929.

the Music Academy was originally founded, on the composer's initiative. This small collection of pianos and memorabilia is set in Liszt's apartment.

The next junction is the **Kodály körönd**, ringed by statues of Hungarian military heroes famed for their exploits against the Turks or the Habsburgs. At No 1 is the **Kodály Memorial Museum**. The last part of Andrássy út features elegant turn-of-the-century villas, many occupied by embassies or foreign businesses. Note the **house of the Federation of Hungarian Journalists**, an Art Nouveau building at No 101.

Hősök tere (Heroes' Square)

The boulevard leads into the huge Heroes' Square, dominated by the **Millennium Monument***, an imposing 38m-high (125ft) column bearing the Archangel Gabriel, by György Zala. Round its base are the same sculptor's evocative equestrian figures, the

The Millennium Monument is the centrepiece, with the Archangel Gabriel triumphantly soaring above Heroes' Square.

The vast neoclassical rooms in the Museum of Fine Arts provide splendid settings for the displays.

Matthias Corvinus's statue takes its place among the great Hungarian rulers in the colonnade around Heroes' Square.

leaders of the seven Magyar tribes. Beyond the column is the pantheon **colonnade of Hungarian rulers**; the choice of statues on display has varied over the years, according to political whims. It now starts with King Stephen and finishes at the right-hand end with Lajos Kossuth.

On the north side of the square is the Greek Revival **Szépművészeti Múzeum★★★** (Museum of Fine Arts, 1906), housing the nation's excellent collection of non-Hungarian art. This ranges from Egyptian, Greek and Roman exhibits, through Renaissance and the Old Masters, to French Impressionists and Post-Impressionists, together with sculptures, drawings and prints. To the south is the **Műcsarnok** (Art Exhibition Hall) of 1896, also Greek Revival and by architects Albert Schickedanz and Fülöp Herzog (who also designed the Museum of Fine Arts). It houses temporary exhibitions. The vast, paved area to the

south (part of **Dózsa György út**) was used for stage-managed Communist rallies and had a mega-statue of Stalin, pulled down to general acclaim by the revolutionaries in 1956; only the giant's boots proved too solid to remove until after the uprising.

Városliget* (City Woodland Park)
Beyond Heroes' Square is the Városliget (City Woodland Park), the site of the millennial celebrations of 1896 marking the conquest of the Carpathian Basin by the Magyars. The park was created from marshland and now forms a 1km-square green oasis for locals and visitors alike, away from the hustle and bustle of the city. In addition, it offers a wide range of recreational facilities. Its most interesting features date from the millennial celebrations, in particular **Vajdahunyad**

The mosaic of St Stephen, patron of the arts, on the pediment of the Art Exhibition Hall was a late addition.

Castle★ on an island in an artificial lake. The castle (a replica of the original castle in Rumania) was the seat of the Hunyadis, built by the mother of Matthias Corvinus and continued by the king himself. Next to it are examples of all the architectural styles to be found in Hungary through the ages, as well as **Miklós Ligeti**'s powerfully romantic statue of *Anonymous,* the author of the first history of the Hungarians and probably a notary at the court of Béla III. The face of this unknown person is hidden under a monkish hood. The Baroque wing houses the **Mezőgazdasági Múzeum** (Agricultural Museum) displaying farm implements, rural crafts and agricultural and country pursuits.

Crossing City Woodland Park from south to north along the shore of the ornamental lake, you come to **Állatkerti körút**, which leads to the **zoo** (*állatkert*). This houses 3 000 animals, from lions and tigers, elephants and hippos to waterfowl and aquarium displays.

At No 2 is the brilliantly revived **Gundel Restaurant**, which maintains both the service and top quality Hungarian cuisine of Károly Gundel, who acquired the restaurant in 1910 and made it internationally famous. A meal here is a memorable experience. To the north is the **circus** and the **amusement park** (immortalised in Ferenc Molnár's *Liliom*, later the musical *Carousel*). To the south is the neo-Baroque **Széchenyi Baths★★★**. In these impressive, very warm and popular baths, you will see locals playing games of floating chess.

Boating on the lake in front of Vajdahunyad Castle, in the City Woodland Park.

From the nearby metro station, take the M1 (yellow) metro to the city centre.

SELECT LIST OF MUSEUMS AND GALLERIES

*The following list covers those museums and galleries mentioned in the text and a few others of local importance. A complete list of museums may be obtained from **Tourinform** at Sütö utca 2.*

Museums close on Mondays (unless otherwise stated below), and have shorter opening hours between October and March. An admission charge is payable but most museums have one day free admission during the week. (The day is noted under individual entries below.) Opening hours are usually between 10am and 6pm (last admissions half an hour before closing).

In the addresses below, the customary Hungarian abbreviations are used: u.=utca (street), krt=körút (boulevard).

Budavári Palota★★★
(Royal Palace Complex) (FV)
Southern end of Castle Hill
See pp.23-27
Wing A: Ludwig Múzeum (Ludwig Collection of Modern Art). Also exhibitions of contemporary history.
Wings B, C, D: Magyar Nemzeti Galéria (Hungarian National Gallery).
Wing E: Budapesti Történéti Múzeum (Budapest History Museum). Includes tour of medieval and Renaissance palace remains. *Closed Tue.*
Wing F: Országos Széchenyi Könyvtár (Széchenyi National Library). Evening opening as well

Ostler statue, Buda Royal Palace.

as daytime hours. Reader's ticket required. *See p.24*
Magyar Nemzeti Múzeum★★
(Hungarian National Museum)
(HX) *Múzeum krt 14-16. Open 10am-6pm. Occasional free concerts. See p.60*
Kiscelli Múzeum
(Kiscelli Museum)
Social history and development of Budapest from the 18C onwards.
Óbuda, Kiscelli u. 108.
Open 10am-6pm.
Néprajzi Múzeum★★
(Ethnographical Museum) (GU)
Kossuth Lajos tér 12. Open 10am-6pm. Free on Tue. See p.73
Iparművészeti Múzeum★★
(Museum of Applied Arts) (HX)
Üllői út 33-37. Open 10am-6pm. Free on Tue. See p.60

Szépművészeti Múzeum★★★
(Museum of Fine Arts)
Hősök tere. Open 10am-6pm.
See p.81

Hadtörténeti Múzeum★
(Museum of Military History) (EU)
Tóth Árpád sétány 40, Castle Hill.
Open Tue-Sun 10am-6pm. See p.34

Közlekedési Múzeum
(Transport Museum)
Városligeti krt, City Woodland Park.
Open 10am-5pm. Free on Wed.
Historic vehicles and the history of
Hungarian railways and transport
systems.

Aquincum Múzeum
(Aquincum Museum)
Szentendrei út 139 (HÉV railway to
Aquincum from Batthyány tér).
Open 10am-6pm. See p.52

Bartók Emlékház
(Béla Bartók Memorial House)
Csalán u. 29. Open 10am-5pm.

Kereskedelmi és Vendéglátóipari
Múzeum (Museum of Commerce
and Catering) (EV)
Fortuna u. 4, Castle Hill.
Open 10am-5pm (6pm on weekends).
See p.36

Kassák Emlékmúzeum
(Lajos Kassák Memorial Museum)
Óbuda, Fő tér 1. Open 10am-6pm.
See p.50

Kodály Múzeum
(Zoltán Kodály Memorial Museum)
Kodály körönd 1. Open Wed 10am-
4pm; Thur-Sat 10am-6pm; Sun
10am-2pm. See p.79

Liszt Ferenc Emlékmúzeum
(Franz Liszt Memorial
Museum) (FU)
Vörösmarty u. 35. Open Mon-Fri
10am-6pm; Sat 9am-5pm. See p.78

Lakásmúzeum
(Zsigmond Kun Collection)
Folk arts collection.
Óbuda, Fő tér 4. Open Tue-Fri 2-6pm;
Sat/Sun 10am-6pm.

Mátyás Templom (Matthias
Church, Ecclesiastical Treasures)
Szentháromság tér, Castle Hill.
Open daily 9.30am-5.30pm. See p.29

Semmelweis Orvostörténeti
Múzeum (Semmelweis Museum of
Medical History) (FV)
Apród u. 1-3. Open 10.30am-6pm.
See p.41

Zsidó Múzeum
(National Jewish Museum) (HV)
Dohány u. 2 (adjacent to the
synagogue). Open Mon-Fri 10am-3pm;
Sun 10am-1pm. See p.63

Evangélikus Országos Múzeum
(National Lutheran Museum)
Deák tér 4. Open 10am-6pm. See p.67

Postamúzeum (Postal Museum)
Andrássy út 3. Open 10am-6pm.
See p.76

Gül Baba Türbéje
(Tomb of Gül Baba)
Mecset u. 14. Open 10am-6pm;
closed Nov-Apr. See pp.46-47

Varga Imre Gyűjtemény
(Imre Varga Sculpture Museum)
Óbuda, Laktanya u. 7 (off Fő tér).
Open 10am-6pm. See p.51

Vasarely Múzeum★
(Victor Vasarely Museum)
Óbuda, Szentlélek tér 1.
Open 10am-6pm. See p.50

Budavári Labirinthus (EU)
Maze of galleries and caves under
Castle Hill.
Úri u. 9.
Open 9.30am-7.30pm. See p.33, 88

A railway line where children are king wends its way through the hills of Buda.

Traditional Hungarian costume.

EXCURSIONS FROM BUDAPEST

Budai-hegység (The Buda Hills)
To the west of the city the delightful Buda Hills offer fresh air and relaxation, as well as a number of interesting places to visit. Children may enjoy a trip on the **Gyermek Vasút★** (Pioneer or Children's Railway) (Bus/Tram 56 from Moszkva tér to Hűvösvölgy). It is operated by children (under supervision, with an adult driver!) and winds up **Széchenyi-hegy** (Széchenyi Hill) on an 11km (7 miles) journey, with five stops from which walking excursions can be made. The nicest, with a magnificent **view**, is **Normafa** (Norma Tree), so-called after an open-air performance of arias from the opera *Norma* that once took place here; it is also a skiing and sledging area in winter. **János-hegy**, the penultimate stop, is the highest point of the Buda Hills (529m/ 1 735ft), and may also be reached via a *libegö* or **chair-lift** (Bus 158 from Moszkva tér to Zugligeti ut). On the top is the **Erzsébet-kilátó** (Elisabeth Look-Out Tower), built in 1910 to a design by Frigyes Schulek.

Alternatively an excursion may be made on the **Fogaskerekü Vasút** (Cogwheel Railway), which leaves from Szilágyi Erzsébet fasor opposite the cylindrical Hotel Budapest (Trams 18, 56 from Moszkva tér). It has nine stops and takes 20 minutes to the summit of **Széchenyi Hill**. On the way it passes the famous **András Pető Institute** for rehabilitating children with motor disabilities, and a Swabian village dating from the time of Maria Theresa.

Also leaving from Moszkva tér, the No 22 bus takes you 8km (5 miles) to the **Budakeszi Vadaspark** (Budakeszi Game

Park), where deer, mouflon and many species of bird roam free. Paths are marked with distances and there are raised areas from where animals can be quietly observed.

A bit more organisation is required to join one of the guided tours of the celebrated **caves** of the Buda Hills, but it is worth the effort. The 7km-long (4.5 miles) **Pálvölgyi cave** is open from April to October. The tour includes the famous stalactites, some of which resemble elephants and crocodiles. There is a network of 10km (6 miles) of caves and tunnels under Castle Hill to be explored. A waxwork exhibition, the **Budavári Labirinthus**, in part of the caves is a gruesome reminder of their use as an air-raid shelter and hospital in the Second World War (see p.33). There are also caves at Castle Hill which are open to the public, and visits to additional caves can be arranged from the ticket offices at Szemlőhegyi and Pálvölgyi caves.

Szoborpark (Sculpture Park)

Some 50 statues of ideological significance were erected in Budapest during the Communist era. The City Council decided in 1990 to relocate them in a custom-built park near the town of Érd, to the west of the capital. The statues of Lenin and Communist luminaries or hacks perhaps look better here than ever they did in the city. Although mostly of the Socialist-Realism style, many of their creators were genuine artists and some of their work (particularly the group sculptures) is undeniably arresting. The park, opened in 1994, is well worth visiting. (*Yellow bus 6 from Kosztolányi Dezső tér to Balatoni út/ Szabadkai út, about 15km/45 mins by bus.*)

This Russian soldier with a flag, like other statues from the Communist era, has been re-erected in the Sculpture Park.

Szentendre★★

The HÉV suburban railway from Batthyány tér (20km/12 miles long) will take you to the delightful artists' colony and former Serbian settlement of Szentendre. Two waves of Serb refugees fled from the Turks and settled here in the 14C and early 17C. The most visible remains of their culture are the marvellous **Orthodox churches**, particularly **Blagovestenska** (possessing a wonderful iconostasis) on **Fő tér★★**; there is usually a background tape of Orthodox chant by a deep-voiced male choir, which enhances the Byzantine atmosphere. Equally fascinating is the **Beograda** (Belgrade Cathedral) at Patriárka utca 5, which, however, can be visited only during Sunday mass. Its precincts include the **Szerb Egyházi Múzeum** (Museum of Serbian Sacred Art).

In the 1920s Szentendre became an Hungarian artists' colony, and still is today. There are many galleries, some associated

Fő tér, the triangular main square in Szentendre, is surrounded by pretty merchants' houses and little cafés and shops.

with the earliest (and often distinguished) colonists (e.g., the Ferenczy family, the head of which was the greatest painter of the celebrated **Nagybánya plein air school of painting**). **Kovács Margit Múzeum★** (Vastagh György utca 1), is devoted to **Margit Kovács** (1902-1977), Hungary's leading ceramic artist of this century, whose works are highly regarded by many, though others may be repelled by their aura of ersatz folk-art, bordering on kitsch. At **Skanzen**, 4km (2.5 miles) to the west, is the Hungarian **open-air museum★** (open only in the summer). It contains ten sections each representing a region of Hungary and with buildings typical of that area, including houses, barns, workshops, mills and churches. Some areas are not yet complete, but it is worth a visit and gives a memorable impression of life in rural Hungary. The local **Tourinform** (Dumtsa Jenő utca 22) can provide information about this and Szentendre in general.

The Danube Bend★★★: Visegrád★★ and Esztergom★★

*A favourite excursion from Budapest, for which there are several bus tours, is that to the **Dunakanyar** (Danube Bend), taking in **Visegrád** and **Esztergom**. During the summer, there are 5-hour boat trips starting from Vigadó tér on the Pest embankment which are particularly scenic, stopping at Szentendre and Visegrád. Public transport provides a good connection (buses from Árpád-híd terminus, Pest side).*

Visegrád★★

Visegrád occupies a strategically important position, perched high on the hill overlooking the bend in the river, so it is not surprising that the Romans occupied the site

The ruins of the palace at Visegrád.

in the 4C (Visegrád means 'elevated fortress'). Visegrád was the summer court of the Hungarian kings from the time of the first Angevin, Károly Robert, until the early 16C. Both the Angevins and Matthias Corvinus spent huge sums on embellishing it, although only a few reconstructions now hint at the palace that so impressed visitors that one of them called it 'a paradise on earth'. In 1335, a summit was held here in an (unsuccessful) attempt to circumvent the monopoly of east-west trade held by Vienna, attended by the Kings of Poland and Bohemia, and the Saxon and Bavarian Dukes.

The former **palace** mostly dates from the time of Matthias Corvinus and its ruins have been enhanced with replicas of the Renaissance **Lion** and **Hercules** fountains that stood here. The **Salomon-torony** (Salomon's Tower) has a small museum, which is perhaps for enthusiasts only, but everyone should make the trek (or take the bus) up to the **Citadel**, with its superb **view★★★** of the Danube far below.

The Basilica in Esztergom is the largest church in Hungary.

Esztergom★★

Historic Esztergom, the seat of the Primate of Hungary, is notable for its neoclassical **Basilica★**, mostly the work of József Hild (1856). It has a fairly chilling interior, where size seems to have been given more weight than aesthetics (the dome is 100m/330ft high, and the copy of Titian's *Assumption* is 13m/42ft by 6.5m/21ft). However, the **Bakócz Chapel** on the left is a gem, rebuilt from the previous cathedral on the site, having been dismantled into 1 600 pieces. The **Keresztény Múzeum★★** has priceless objects from as early as the 9C. The nearby medieval **Royal Castle** is the birthplace of St Stephen.

Kecskemét** and the Alföld

No trip to Hungary is complete without an excursion to the **Alföld** (Great Hungarian Plain). The major town of the central-southern plain is **Kecskemét**★★, a centre of agricultural commerce spared the worst ravages of the Turks. The star attraction is Ödön Lechner's **Városháza**★ (Town Hall). The frescoes by Bertalan Székely in the ornate Council Chamber include a striking depiction of *The Magyar Clans Taking the Blood Oath of Allegiance to Árpád*, thought to have taken place at Pusztaszer, not far to the south.

Near Kecskemét, the traditional skills of horsemanship of the herdsmen of the Great Plain may be seen at **Lajosmisze** and **Bugac**. Package tours here usually include a display of acrobatic riding, the running of half-breds past the spectators and sightseeing of animals and related crafts. A goulash lunch in a *csárdá*, with romantic fiddling, complete the romantic image of life in the Great Plain, which was, in reality, cruel and hard.

Sheep grazing the Puszta Plains.

ENJOYING YOUR VISIT

SPIRIT OF BUDAPEST

To get the most out of the Magyar capital, why not follow in the footsteps of its inhabitants and head for the spa, bright and early in the morning? Wearing a beautiful blue bathing cap, you can roam through the fabulous setting, jumping from a pool of very hot water to an icy cold one, before being covered with oil and given a vigorous and unforgettable massage by a giant sporting an exraordinary moustache ... unless you prefer to remain calm but alert by partaking in the national pastime that consists in paddling around in front of a floating chessboard.

Now that you're feeling invigorated but perhaps a bit peckish, it's time to hit the galleries at **Vásárcsarnok**, Pest's central market, with its stalls bursting with fruits and vegetables, wreaths of paprika, strings of salami, jars of *foie gras*, wines and brandies. Try a small glass of *barackpálinka*, apricot schnapps, or have a taste of 'black soup', the strong coffee that is a legacy from the Turks.

Then again, you might want to treat yourself to a snack at one of the city's legendary **cafés**, where the setting alone can whisk you off into another age, whether it's the **Café Mozart** with its costumed staff, the **Gerbeaud** that has preserved its 1900s atmosphere, the Viennese café at the **Gellért Hotel**, or the **New York** café and its unfogettable Rococo décor. The Central European aura is further enhanced by the profusion of pastries that are a delight to gourmands of all ages: from the national dessert, *palacsinta*, or crepes with filling, to *réteo*, strudels filled with apples, poppy seeds or curd-cheese, and *somlói galuska*, whose name 'sponge cake' translates its richness but not its infinite subtlety, not to mention the delicious mocha-flavoured *Dobos torta*. In short, depending on your point of view, it's either paradise or hell!

Living Budapest to the fullest means getting out and about, where you can play with this language that seems to have 'come from afar' and appears to take great pleasure in using a bost of most imporbable accents. It means spending hours going from old Europe marked by its thousand-year-old history, to the pompous constructions so dear to the Austrian Hapsburgs, the unbridled whimsy of the Secessionist Art Nouveau buildings, and vestiges from the Ottoman era that have marked both the city itself and its spirit. It means roaming through the silent streets of old Buda that seems to be from another age, or strolling down Pest's lively walking streets around Váci utca, with their jugglers and tumblers, and their enticing shop window displays. It means hopping from underground (the oldest in Europe!) to tramway, or taking a boat ride down the mythical Danube, which really is blue here at times.

And, yes, experiencing Budapest also means bowing to tradition: dining at a restaurant where, after having a few *pogácsa* (*brioches*) for appetisers, you might order the inescapable *pörkölt* (goulash), unless you prefer to try the *csülök* (ham hocks) or the *paprikás csirke* (chicken paprika). After a glass of the Tokay Aszú or Balaton cabernet, as a glow comes into your eyes and you lose the thread of the conversation, the scratchy, heart-rending sound of a Gypsy violin adds a melancholy note to the festivities. Without you realising it, Budapest has been working its subtle magic.

WEATHER

Hungary has a continental climate, producing extremely warm summers with temperatures over 30°C (86°F) in July and August, and bitterly cold winters, with daytime temperatures often below freezing for much of January.

Spring and autumn are the most pleasant seasons for tourism, in particular September and October, when

there are often long periods of mild weather. Budapest is not especially romantic in winter – Pest is disfigured by the dirty slush following any significant snowfall. In very cold years the Danube may contain ice-flows, picturesque to the viewer, but dangerous to shipping. Interiors tend to be overheated in winter, partly a consequence of ancient central heating systems.

CALENDAR OF EVENTS

31 December-1 January: New Year festivities take place all over town; a suitable gala performance is held at the Pesti Vigadó, such as *Die Fledermaus.*

February: The Budapest Carnival, *Farsang* (usually on the last weekend), is marked by a carnival, street parades and other events.

March: Budapest Spring Festival is primarily a festival of classical music, but also includes opera, ballet and folk dance. The annual Art Expo of modern art coincides with this festival.

15 March: Anniversary of the 1848 uprising against the Austrians, marked with rallies and speeches.

Easter: Very important in Hungary and a chance for the churches to bring out their treasures and historic emblems. Processions in traditional costumes are also a feature. The village fertility custom ('dowsing' of girls) occurs even in the city, albeit in a somewhat debased form.

1 May: A public holiday with many festivities in the city parks, particularly those such as the Népliget (People's Park) associated with the working classes rather than the bourgeoisie.

June-August: Budapest Summer, with various concerts, theatrical and musical events.

30 June: Celebration of the withdrawal of Soviet troops in 1991.

August: Summer opera and ballet festival.

20 August: St Stephen's Day, marking the foundation of a Christian Hungarian state. Folk art fairs, sports events and a dramatic fireworks display from the Gellért Hill in the evening.

September: Budapest Wine Festival, with tastings, stalls and a parade.

September/October: Budapest Arts Weeks, with music, theatre and dance events throughout the city.

23 October: National Holiday, marking the outbreak of the 1956 Revolution.

25/26 December: Christmas – for Hungarians, Christmas Eve is more important, a day sacred to the family. Public transport stops at 4pm.

The Gellért Hotel, with its spa and thermal baths, is one of Budapest's leading hotels.

ACCOMMODATION

As in any city, accommodation ranging from the luxurious to the very basic can be found in Budapest. Places to stay include hotels, pensions, inns, motels and private rooms. The Hungarian Tourist Board publishes two brochures annually, one of which lists Hotels, Pensions and Tourist Hostels, the other camp sites, ☎ 317 9800 Fax 317 9656 (*see* pp.125-126 for addresses).

Booking in advance is advisable, particularly if you require mid-priced accommodation during the peak season. Booking a flight and hotel package through a travel agent usually offers the best deal.

In general, the international star rating applies, with 5-star ranking highest, but standards and prices can vary quite widely. A rough guide to prices per room is as follows (single rates tend to be the same as those for double rooms):

5-star: 40 000Ft
4-star: 30 000Ft–40 000Ft
3-star: 19 000Ft–30 000Ft
2-star: 16 000Ft–19 000Ft
1-star: up to 16 000Ft

Facilities in the 5-star hotels are on a par with Europe's best, but further down the scale expectations should be a little lower. Private rooms are cheaper still, but some facilities may be shared.

Paprika is a key ingredient in many traditional Hungarian dishes.

Tourist hostels are the cheapest places to stay, graded A and B depending on the number of beds per room and whether or not there is hot water. Some are official International Youth Hostels, for which international membership is required.

Recommendations

Several hotels offer the ultimate in luxury, and in good locations, but they will be beyond the budgets of most travellers. They include the **Hilton** (Hess András ter 1-3 ☎ 214 3000), **Inter-Continental** (Apáczai Csere János u. 12-14 ☎ 327 6333), **Hyatt Regency** (Roosevelt tér 2 ☎ 266 1234) and the **Grand Hotel Corvinus Kempinski** (Ersébet tér 7-8 ☎ 429 3777).

Among spa hotels the most famous is the **Gellért** (Szent Gellért tér 1 ☎ 185 2200), but there are two on Margaret Island (both expensive), the **Thermal** (☎ 329 2300) or the

☎ 274 4000) which is simple
but well-kept.

More affordable
accommodation can be found
at the **Papillon Hotel**
(Rózsahegy u. 3b ☎ 212 4750)
on the Hill or Roses, or the
Délibáb Hotel (Délibáb u. 35
☎ 322 8763), located inside a
townhouse which, although
noisy, has the advantage of
being near the centre of Pest.

If sleeping on board a boat
on the Danube, rather than
cruising it, is your dream,
Dunapart (☎ 355 9001),
moored across from the
Parliament, can make your
dream come true.

FOOD AND DRINK

Hungarian cuisine is known for
its spicy flavours with red chilli,
onions, tomatoes and peppers –
compatible ingredients served
in substantial portions – such as
the famous goulasch soup
(*gulyas*) and paprika chicken.
Such dishes are often cooked in
goose fat. This rather stodgy fare
is, apparently, gradually being
replaced, with sunflower oil
ousting lard and fresh salads
and home-cooking becoming
much more widespread.

Soup (*leves*) is an important
element in Hungarian cuisine –
gulyásleves is the most common
way of eating goulash, and is a
meal in itself. Soup takes many

Danubius Grand Hotel (☎ 452
5800).

Less expensive, but offering
traditional style and Art
Nouveau decor, are the
Mercure Nemzeti (Jósef krt. 4
☎ 477 2000) and the **Astoria**
(Kossuth Lajos u. 19-21 ☎ 317
3411). The modern **Mercure
Korona** (Kecskeméti u. 14
☎ 317 4111) has a good
location and facilities.

For more moderate
accommodation, try the
centrally located **Victoria** (Bem
Rakpart 11 ☎ 457 8080), or the
Queen Mary (Béla Király u. 47

Tasty sausages make an excellent picnic lunch.

root vegetables, smoked pork and dumplings, as well as beans. In summer, *hideg meggyleves* (cold Morello cherry soup) is popular.

Of **cold appetisers** (*hideg előételek*), the famous *libamáj* (goose liver) is worth trying, with a chilled white wine. **Warm starters** (*meleg előételek*) tend to include mushrooms or cheese unadventurously fried in breadcrumbs (*gombafejek rántva, rántott sajt*); but *hortobágyi palacsinta*, meat-filled crêpes similar to cannelloni, are usually good.

Hungary has a great tradition of freshwater **fish**, the most famous being the zander (*fogás*) indigenous to Lake Balaton. It has a delicate taste and is cooked in many different ways – Kalocsa style with *lecsó* (stewed onions, paprika and tomatoes), à la Gundel (with spinach and cheese sauce), or simply grilled in fillets. Carp (*ponty*) is usually fried in breadcrumbs or boiled, while the *süllő* (a young zander with very soft, white flesh) is usually grilled.

forms, but a speciality to look out for is *halászlé* (paprika-spiced fish soup made from different kinds of freshwater fish, chiefly carp). Vegetable soups are almost always good (and filling), a particularly tasty one being *Jókai bableves* (Jókai bean soup), which contains

Chicken or **turkey** breasts (*csirkemell, pulykamell*) are frequently on the menu, often cooked in 'Parisian style' (with ham and cheese and fried in breadcrumbs). An old standby is *paprikás csirke* (paprika chicken), tender chicken strongly spiced and stewed. For a treat try the *kacsa* (crispy roast duck stuffed with a quince).

When it comes to **meat**, the ubiquitous Wiener Schnitzel turns up in Hungary as *rántott sertészelet* (the pork version), or *rántott borjúszelet* (veal). Pork (*sertés*) may be braised (*brassói aprópecsenye*), pan-fried slices (*cigány pecsenye*), or stewed (*pörkölt*); *pörkölt* is common on menus and could equally well consist of beef (*marha*), veal (*borjú*) or lamb (*birka*). If you like onions, *hagymás rostély* (pan-fried beef with crispy onions) is tasty.

Vegetables as a side-dish in Hungary are usually a sad affair of tasteless chopped morsels or lacklustre salads. On the other hand, vegetable-based dishes are good, in the Balkan tradition. Stuffed paprika (*töltött paprika*) or stuffed cabbage (*töltött káposzta*) are often available. Vegetables thickened in roux and sour cream (*főzelék*) can be delicious (*karalábefőzelék*/kohlrabi, *parajfőzelék*/spinach, *lencsefőzelék*/lentils and *babfőzelék*/beans). Potatoes come as *hasábburgonya* (fried), *fött krumpli* (boiled), *sült krumpli* (roast) or *püré* (purée).

Salads (*saláták*), often pickles (*savanyúság*), tend to be drenched in vinegar.

Sauerkraut (*káposztasaláta*) goes well with the fattier dishes and *uborkasaláta* (thinly sliced cucumber sprinkled with red pepper) is also recommended.

Konditorei or café often sell the most appealing **desserts**. Standbys in restaurants are the *palacsinták* (pancakes), the best being the Gundel version with chocolate sauce and walnuts – sometimes flambéed, and the really excellent one with sweet curds (*túróspalacsinta*). **Pastry**-lovers will go wild in Budapest, with creations from a long-standing tradition where pastry chefs go all out (flaky pastry came from the Ottomans). Specialities include *Rigó Jancsi*, a chocolate and whipped cream pastry, hundreds of kinds of strudels (*réteo*), *Túró Rudi*, curd cheese topped with chocolate, and *somlói galuska*, sponge cake with walnuts, raisins, chocolate sauce and whipped cream.

Drinks (*Italok*) The standard Hungarian aperitif is *pálinka*, usually *barackpálinka* (apricot schnapps), a fiery and aromatic liquid that stimulates the appetite; the best comes from Kecskemét on the Great Plain. A good digestive is *Unicum*, a famous Hungarian firm dating back to the turn of the century, and restored to family ownership.

Local mineral water is, of course, abundant. **Beer** (*sör*) is widely available in bottles and, to a lesser extent, in cans. Budapest's Kőbánya brewery, and indeed most of Hungary's brewers, are in Austrian or German hands. *Csapolt sör* (draught beer) is therefore likely to be one of the well-known European (or Scandinavian) brands, but some bars do offer local, light, frothy beer such as *Dreher* and *Kaiser*, served in big (*korso*) or small (*pohar*) mugs. Excellent Czech beer is also quite widely available.

Mass production of heavily doctored and homogenized **wine** almost ruined the reputation of the Hungarian wine industry under Socialism, but things have improved since

1990. Sophisticated viticulture is now undertaken, with investment and expertise supplied by France, Italy, Australia and from elsewhere. Avoid the cheaper generic wines and go for wines with a clearly indicated provenance. Prices for these wines are much higher (typically starting at around 900 Ft a bottle), but are usually worth the extra.

The typical wine of Hungary is white and tending to sweetness, although there are excellent dry whites and interesting reds as well. White wines are grown all over the country, but especially around Lake Balaton, from where come excellent Sauvignons, Italian Riesling (*Olaszrizling*), and *Szürkebarát* (Pinot Gris). Peter Zwack, of Unicum fame, has

There are some good local wines to choose from.

A cocktail coming up in the Gundel restaurant.

teamed up with French investors to produce wonderful wines from the estate of Bátaapáti Kastély, notably a first-rate *Zöldveltelini* (Grüner Veltliner). White wines (*Furmint, Hárslevelű/* Lindenblatt) are blended in the famous **Tokay** (*Tokaji*) dessert wine from the northern hills.

The tasting of *Tokay* 'the wine of kings and and king of wines,' as Louis XIV said, is one of the world's most sensual wine experiences. Shrouded in myth and legend, it was believed to possess the miraculous powers of an elixir of life. Look for

Tokay marked Aszú, indicating the addition of grapes with the 'noble rot'. The wine is graded by '*puttonyos*' – literally 'barrels'. The more *puttonyos*, the better the wine – but the more costly.

Some of the best red wines come from the Villány region in the south, such as *Kékfrankos* (Blaufränkisch), *Cabernet Sauvignon* and *Merlot*. An interesting native grape is the *Kadarka,* mostly from the Szekszárd region. Perhaps the best-known Hungarian red is Bikaver, 'Bull's Blood', from the ancient town of Eger, to the north.

103

Recommendations

Cafés (*Kávéházak*) and **Konditoreien** (*cukrászdak*) offer coffee – in Budapest it is usually very strong – and a wide selection of pastries and sticky cakes, as well as sandwiches. The best places, for example the **Jégbüfé** on Kossuth Lajos utca, have fresh supplies from their own bakeries.

Many of the old cafés have died out in Budapest, but a select few soldier on, some having been renovated through fresh investment. The **New York** (Erzsébet körút) is always popular (*see* p.62). Nice renovations include the **Múzeum**, next to the National Museum, and the **Művész cukrászda** on Andrássy út. The famous *Konditoreien*, **Gerbeaud** on Vörösmarty tér in Pest and **Ruszwurm** on Castle Hill, are thriving. And don't miss **Lukács** on Andrássy út which is packed with pastry-lovers, or **Angelika** (Batthyány ter, in Buda, along the Danube).

Restaurants range from the luxurious to friendly and informal establishments offering home cooking; a classic example is **Náncsi Néni Vendéglője ☎ 397 2742**, reached by Bus 57 to Ördögárok út 80. In many restaurants frequented by tourists there is live music,

The Gundel restaurant, in the City Woodland Park, is as popular today as it was before the Socialist era.

Hand-embroidered articles for sale in a market.

ranging from traditional Hungarian and gypsy music to pop. The world-famous **Gundel** (Állat kerti út. 2 ☎ 321 3550) is expensive, and booking is essential, as is the case for the equally expensive **Robinson** (Városliget tó ☎ 343 3776), which is housed in a converted vaulted chapel. For more moderately-priced eating try the **Kehli Vendeglö** (Mokus u. 22 ☎ 250 4241), in a picturesque setting, or the **Apostolok** (Kigyó u. 4-6 ☎ 318 3559) an old vaulted chapel with wooden carvings. The **Kisbuda Gyöngye** (Kenyeres utca 34 ☎ 368 6402) is also good value with local atmosphere and well-prepared dishes. The **Belcanto** (Dalszinhaz utca 8 ☎ 269 2786), next to the Opera, is very original with the waiters and chefs encouraging sing-alongs. Good quality food is also served. Those who aren't scared off by the name, which refers to the wooden boards that dishes are served on, can try out **Fatál** (Váci u. 67, entrance on Pintér u. ☎ 342 2587). A Tzigane atmosphere reigns at **Regi Sipos Halászkert** (Lajos u. 46 ☎ 368 6480).

It is worth consulting the listings in the two English language newspapers available at news kiosks, *The Budapest Sun* and *Budapest Week*. A helpful local publication is Sam Worthington's *The Dreher Good Living Guide to Hungary* (though irregularly updated).

SHOPPING

At Pest, there are several very commercial avenues such as Rakoczi út or try shopping around Váci utca and Kigyo utca (GV) where there are many boutiques selling Hungarian specialities and most Western goods. Popular souvenirs include Transylvanian embroidery, Herend pottery, and gastronomic items such as Tokay wine, salami, goose liver pâté and *barackpálinka*. Shops on Castle Hill offer folk art and souvenirs ranging from the appealing to the indescribably awful. Chess sets are popular, reflecting the nation's passion for the game.

Recommendations

A good selection of Hungarian wines can be found at **Wine City** (Párizsi u. 1, Pest). The **Folkart Centrum** at Váci u. 14 (and a further eight shops around the city) specialise in folk arts. A good bookshop with books in non-Hungarian languages covering all aspects of the country's history and culture is **Litea** (in the Fortuna Passage, Hess András tér 4, Castle Hill). In Pest, there are books in English (also on Hungarian topics) at **Bestsellers** (Október 6 u. 11). CDs and records can be bought at **Hungaroton** on Vörösmarty tér, which has a large classical department featuring Hungarian composers and performers. The world-famous Herend porcelain, can be found in **Herend Porcelain** (József Nádor tér 11). You can also visit the **Duna Plaza**, a large, modern shopping centre, offering a wide range of wares and local delicacies (Metro 3, Blue line; station: Gyöngyösi).

ENTERTAINMENT AND NIGHTLIFE

An evening **cruise** on the Danube within Budapest at night, when many of the main sights are illuminated, can be a very attractive and romantic way to explore the city. Taking about an hour and a half, they depart from Vigadó tér quay.

Music in Budapest is rich and

The Ybl Várkert Kiosk has been beautifully restored and converted into a casino-restaurant.

varied, ranging from gypsy music and folk dancing, through rock and jazz to opera. Most evenings there is a choice of concerts in the Music Academy, opera in the Állami Operaház (State Opera House) and chamber concerts in attractive venues such as the Erdődy Palace or the Dominican Cloister of the Hilton Hotel, on Castle Hill. The Budapest Spring Festival offers various events over ten days.

The **National Philharmonia Ticket Office** on Vörösmarty tér supplies complete listings of forthcoming performances and also sells tickets for most of them, as do IBUSZ on

Ferencíek tere and other tourist offices. *The Budapest Sun* and *Budapest Week* have listings of the many films shown in English (also French, German and Italian).

Folk music (including performances by *Muszikás*, Hungary's most popular folk group) can be heard at the **Fővárosi Művelödési Ház** at Fehérvári út 47, while the splendid shows of the Hungarian State Folk Ensemble take place at the Budai Vigadó, Corvin tér 8.

Operetta fans can enjoy a pot-pourri concert of hits in the **Pesti Vigadó** (Vigadó tér 2). An unusual outing is an evening river cruise with a sound and light show, organised by Legenda Kft., Frankó u. 4 (or enquire at the Mahart Office on Vigadó tér).

Nightlife is now extremely lively, with many jazz clubs, discos, music bars and nightclubs. It is advisable to check the English language press listings, but you may like to try: **Merlin Jazz Club and English Language Theatre**, at Gerlóczy u.4 (live music with dinner and occasional performances of Hungarian works in English), **Jazz Café** at Balassi Bálint u. 25 (live music),

and the **Béke Radisson Hotel** (Teréz krt 43), which has probably the best traditional floorshow, with dinner also served. For a final drink, maybe try **Beckett's Irish Pub** (Bajcsy-Zsilinsky u. 72), which has live music at the weekend, or the **Irish Cat Pub** (Muzeum krt 41) where you can dine and drink. You may prefer the attractive marine decor of the **Fregatt** (Molnar u. 26), or you can dance the night away at the **Bahnhof Marlboro Music Club V** (VIe, Váci u. 1), from Wednesday to Saturday 9pm-

Ice skating in City Woodland Park is a popular winter pastime.

4am – a discotheque with good but slightly dated rock music. The **Stage Pub** (Ve, Aranykez u. 5) is the first internet pub in Budapest, open to 2am, you can have a drink or surf on the net in a relaxed atmosphere.

SPORTS

As an alternative to spa-based activities, the city has **tennis**, **squash** and **bowling**, whilst **horse-riding** is available just outside Budapest. **Golf** is relatively new to Hungary, but there is a course on Szentendre Island. **Ice skating** in City Woodland Park is popular in winter, as is **skiing** on János Hill.

For spectators, one of the main events of the year is the **Formula I Grand Prix** at Hungaroring (19km/12 miles east of Budapest). **Football** is the most popular spectator sport, with international games held at the Népstadion (which also hosts other sporting events). **Horse-racing** is also popular with locals (flat racing at Lóverseny tér galopp-pálya, X, Albertirsai út 2; trotting races at Ugetö-pálya, VIII, Kerepesi út 11).

There are a number of **swimming pools** in the city: the Palatinus Baths, on Margaret Island, are very popular with the young; the Alfred Hajós Baths, also on the island, offer excellent facilities for serious swimmers and divers; the Csillaghegy Open Air Bath, with its coolish water and attractive parkland, is an ideal refuge on hot August afternoons.

For an unforgettable souvenir of your visit, why not fly over Budapest in a hot air balloon: 365 days of the year, weather permitting, contact Sup-Air Balloon Club ☎ **322 0015**.

Thermal Springs and Spas

Budapest has no fewer than 123 thermal springs, producing around 50 million litres of warm, mineral-rich water a year. The earliest settlers of Budapest recognised the healing properties of the water, and the springs were probably the reason the earliest inhabitants settled on Gellért Hill. Later, the Romans were quick to exploit this plentiful supply of water, which ranges in temperature from 24–70°C (75–158°F), and used them to supply their baths, the remains of which can be seen in Budapest today. The settlement was called Aquincum, 'Abundant Waters'.

The Magyars also took advantage of the thermal waters, and travellers came to sample the waters for themselves. Later, in the Middle Ages, the Knights Hospitallers of St John founded hospitals based on spas, notably on the sites of the Géllert and Lukács baths. For the Turks, in the 16C and 17C, bathing was an important ritual and many of today's spas date from this time.

The discovery of further springs in the 19C and the building of new establishments such as the neo-Baroque Széchenyi Baths led to another surge in Budapest's popularity as a health spa. Today, they form a central part of life for most locals, who regard the

The outdoor pool at Gellért Spa is fed by warm natural springs.

baths much as the Romans did – a place to socialise, relax and soak away the cares of the day.

The thermal waters are used to treat a range of disorders, including circulation, rheumatism, gynaecological, metabolic and nervous system problems.The range of treatments is equally diverse, including thermal, tub and steam baths, massage, mud baths, electro-therapy and drinking cures.

Select List of Baths and Spas

Opening times vary, but all the spas and pools listed below are open between about 6.30am and 6pm on weekdays and between about

6.30am and noon at weekends. Some open well beyond these times and there are generally shorter opening periods in winter. There is a rule, in most baths, that bathing caps must be worn (plastic ones are obtainable at the cash desk for a small fee). There are 32 baths in Budapest, ten of which are recognised as health spas. A selection is listed below.

Gellért Gyógyfürdő (Gellért Spa, Szent Gellért tér 1) (GX) The most luxurious – but touristy. Facilities range from teeth cleaning to a wave bath (in summer).

Király Gyógyfürdő (Király Baths, Fö utca 84) Attractive Turkish baths dating to the 16C. Men only Mon, Wed, Fri; women only Tue, Thur, Sat. Closed Sun.

Lukács Gyógyfürdő (Lukács Baths, Frankel Leó út) Civilised, old-fashioned; nice sun terrace for summer and one bracing cold bath.

Rudas Gyógyfürdő (Rudas Baths, Döbrentei tér 9) (GX) This (and the nearby **Rác Baths** (Hadnagy utca 8-10), said to have been used by Kings Sigismund and Mátyás) offer the genuine Turkish experience.

Széchenyi Gyógyfürdő (Széchenyi Baths, Állakerti körut 11) Situated in City Wood-land Park, this popular complex exploits the hot waters (70°C at source) of the Városliget.

THE BASICS

Before You Go

All visitors entering Hungary need a valid passport. Nationals from the UK, most European countries, Canada and the US do not need a visa when visiting for a period up to three months. A visa is required by citizens of Australia, New Zealand and most non-European countries. For information about visa requirements, contact the Hungarian Embassy Consular Department, 35b Eaton Place, London SW1 X8BY ☎ **020 7235 5218**; the Hungarian Consulate, 102 Bloor St West, Suite 1001, Toronto, Ontario M55 1M8 ☎ **416 333 3302**; or the Hungarian National Tourism Office, 33rd Floor, 150 E. 58th Street, New York, NY 10155 ☎ **212 355 0240**.

No vaccinations are necessary, although anybody diagnosed as having an infectious disease may not enter the country.

Getting There

Budapest Ferihegy, Hungary's international airport, has three terminals, situated 20-24km (12-15 miles) south-east of the city. Terminal 1 handles all flights from Eastern Europe, Terminal 2 is used by **MALÉV** (Hungarian Airlines) and most other airlines, and Terminal 3 is used by private aircraft.

Various international airlines operate flights to Budapest from over 30 countries and MALÉV operate scheduled flights to over 40 foreign cities.

There are three international railway stations in Budapest: Budapest Eastern (Keleti), Budapest Western (Nyugati) and Budapest Southern (Déli) where Eurocity (EC) and Intercity (IC) trains arrive daily from Frankfurt, Berlin, Belgrade, Rijeka, Vienna, Dortmund, Prague and Warsaw. Visitors from London travel via Dover, Ostend and Vienna. The Orient Express runs from Paris, but advance booking is essential. In addition, over 50 international scheduled trains, all with dining and sleeping cars, arrive per day. Information on international trains is available on ☎ **342 9150** and ☎ **322 4052** daily, from 6am-8pm or **461 5500** (24hrs); ☎ **461 5400** (domestic).

Volánbusz Transport Company operates an international bus service several countries, including Great Britain; services from western countries arrive at the Erzsébet tér bus terminal (☎ **317 2562**), while those from the east and south arrive at the terminal beside Népstadion (☎ **252 1896**). Information about timetables and prices is available Monday to Saturday on the numbers given.

A hydrofoil service operates on the River Danube between Budapest and Vienna, with a stop at Bratislava.

To enter Hungary by car motorists need the documents detailed under **Driving** (*see* p.119). Border crossings on the main roads are open 24 hours a day, but the smaller ones close at midnight.

Arriving

The best way to get into the city from the airport is on the LRI minibus, which leaves every 30 minutes for Erzsébet tér bus terminal, stopping at the main hotels, and is reasonably priced. For the return journey you can order an Airport Minibus on (☎ **296 8555**). It is best to avoid taxis as the prices are unregulated and tend to be very high. If you do travel by taxi, agree the fee beforehand.

The Western Station was designed by Gustave Eiffel, 1874-1877.

A-Z

Accidents and Breakdowns

If you are in a hire car, the rental company should be able to assist you, so carry their details with you at all times.

Emergency phones are located every 2km (1 mile) along the M7 motorway and the No 5 main highway and help can be sought 24 hours a day from the emergency telephones in towns.

The Hungarian Auto Club operates a mobile service known as 'Yellow Angels' because of the colour of their vehicles. Their phone number in all areas of the country is ☎ **088**.

If your car cannot be repaired on the spot, they will arrange to have it towed away for you. The Hungarian Auto Club also operates an International Aid Service for foreign motorists which includes emergency help, towing, technical advice and letters of credit ☎ **212 2821**.

In the event of an accident, the police must be informed initially, and you should also call the Hungária Insurance Company, 1113 Budapest, Hamzsabég út 60 ☎ **209 0703** ext 250-4 Mon-Fri 8am-4pm.

Airports see **Getting There p.112**

Banks

The National Bank of Hungary, Budapest V, Szabadság tér 8, is open from 10.30am to 2pm, Monday to Friday. The commercial banks are open from 8am to 3pm, Monday to Thursday and from 8am to 1pm on Fridays. All banks are closed on Saturday. Automatic currency exchange machines and automatic cash dispensers (ATM) operate after hours. When exchanging money or travellers' cheques in banks, you will need to produce your passport. *See also* **Money**

Bicycles

Bikes can be hired for the day or week fairly easily in Budapest, although you may have to shop around for lighter-weight models with several gears. Beware of cobbled streets and tram lines. Contact TOURINFORM, Sütő utca, 2, 1052 Budapest (close to Deák tér metro station) ☎ **317 9800**, fax 317 9656 for more details.

Books

George Konrád *The Case Worker* and *The City Builder* Two documentary and philosophical novels, evoking the human and physical environment of an anonymous Eastern European city, which is in fact Konrád's native Budapest.

Ferenc Molnár *The Paul Street Boys* A juvenile classic set at the turn of the century, much enjoyed by adults as well as children. This is the touching story of two gangs of boys and their battle over a piece of wasteland in Pest.

John Bierman *Righteous Gentile* The best account of Raoul Wallenberg, the heroic Swedish consul who saved many Jews from the Nazis as the Germans prepared to ship them from the Budapest ghetto to the camps in 1944-1945.

Péter Hanák(ed.) *One Thousand Years – A Concise*

Miklós Ligeti's statue of Anonymous, Vajdahunyad Castle.

History of Hungary A concise and digestible, yet accurate, history of Hungary. David Irving *Uprising!* An exciting account of the 1956 revoution, based on hundreds of eyewitness accounts and interviews with participants on both sides. György Litván(ed.) *The Hungarian Revolution of 1956* A definitive record of 1956, measured, authoritative and comprehensive. Incorporates material from formerly closed Communist archives in Budapest and Moscow. John Lukács *Budapest 1900*

A vivid cultural study of the great metropolis on the brink of 20C tragedies.

Budapest Card (Kártya)

We highly recommend these passes, which can be purchased at TOURINFORM, and at the airport, major underground stations and travel agencies.

The passes are valid for two days (2 800Ft) or three days (3 400Ft). They give you unlimited access to public transport (underground, buses, trolley-cars, tramways and HÉV suburban trains) within the city (beyond which a supplement is required).

In addition, you get free admission to most museums and cultural sites and can obtain discounts in certain shops, for car hire (Budget) or bicycle hire on Margaret Island. The accompanying booklet lists all the benefits.

Camping

There are a number of campsites within reach of Budapest, details of which can be obtained from TOURINFORM. They range from first-class, complete with shops and restaurants, to third class which, although with far fewer facilities, may be more natural and peaceful. Certain sites offer reductions to members of the International Camping and Caravanning Club (FICC). Children under 14 are also entitled to reductions. Camping off-site is illegal.

Trams are a popular form of transport in the city.

Car Hire

A car is not really the best way of getting around Budapest as public transport is convenient and reasonably priced. Having said that, the major car-hire firms have offices in Hungary and cars can either be booked from your own country in advance or from certain travel agencies and hotel desks in Budapest.

Drivers must be over 21 and have held a full licence for at least a year. Ensure that you have valid insurance and check the tyres (including the spare), the horn and brakes before setting off.

Children

Budapest offers a wealth of children's entertainment, with the zoo, circus and amusement park among the attractions likely to appeal to them.

Children under six travel free on public transport and those under 14 pay 50 per cent of the full fare.

Baby products are available in department stores and larger supermarkets. A useful book is Bob Dent's locally-published *Budapest for Children* (1992).

Clothing

Hungary, like the rest of Central Europe, has extremely hot summers and extremely cold winters, so plan accordingly. Most Hungarian shoe and clothes sizes follow the standard current throughout Europe, but differ from those in the UK and US. The following are examples:

Dress Sizes

UK	8	10	12	14	16	18
Europe	34	36	38	40	42	44
US	6	8	10	12	14	16

Men's Suits

UK & US	36	38	40	42	44	46
Europe	46	48	50	52	54	56

Men's Shirts

UK & US	14	14.5	15	15.5	16	16.5	17
Europe	36	37	38	39/40	41	42	43

Men's Shoes

UK	7	7.5	8.5	9.5	10.5	11
Europe	41	42	43	44	45	46
US	8	8.5	9.5	10.5	11.5	12

Women's Shoes

UK	4.5	5	5.5	6	6.5	7
Europe	38	38	39	39	40	41
US	6	6.5	7	7.5	8	8.5

Complaints

Complaints about goods or services should ideally be made at the time. At a hotel or restaurant, make your complaint in a calm manner to the manager. If matters are not dealt with to your satisfaction, or for more serious complaints, report your problem to the tourist office or, in the worst cases, to the police.

A-Z FACTFINDER

Consulates and Embassies

Australia Királyhágó tér 8-9, H-1126 Budapest, ☎ 201 8899
Canada Budakeszi utca 32, Budapest, H-1121 ☎ 275 1200
New Zealand Terez krt 38, H-1066 Budapest ☎ 331 4908
UK Harmincad utca 6, H-1051 Budapest, ☎ 266 2888, or ☎ 06 601 4542 (after office hours)
US V Szabadság tér 12, H-1054 Budapest, ☎ 267 4400, or ☎ 111 9600 (after office hours).

Crime

Unfortunately, petty crime, such as pick-pocketing and breaking into cars, is on the increase in Budapest. It is advisable to carry as little money, and as few credit cards, as possible, and to leave any valuables in the hotel safe. Carry wallets and purses in secure pocket or wear a money belt, and carry handbags across your body or firmly under your arm.

Never leave your car unlocked, and hide away or remove, items of value.

If you do have anything stolen, report it immediately to the local police ☎ 107. If your passport is stolen, report it immediately to the consulate or embassy. *See* **Consulates** .

Currency *see* **Money**

Customs and Entry Regulations

Personal effects relevant to your stay in Hungary can be taken in duty free and anyone over 16 can take in 250 cigarettes, 2 litres of wine and 1 litre of spirits.

If you have any jewellery or equipment of great value, or if you are taking in currency exceeding 50 000Ft when exchanged, it is advisable to ask for a 'Certificate of Valuables Entered' to avoid any dispute when you leave.

To take objects of cultural value out of the country, an export permit is required. Contact TOURINFORM about how to go about this.

Disabled Visitors

In general, facilities for the disabled in Budapest are not widespread. Public transport and access to many public buildings can pose real problems and staying anywhere other than in one of the new, large hotels is likely to be out of the question. However, the National Federation of the Association of Disabled People, San Marco utca 76, can give advice and information, as can TOURINFORM.

Holidays and Travel Abroad: A Guide to Europe is available from RADAR, 12 City Forum, 250

City Road, London EC1V 8AF ☎ **020 7250 3222** between 10am and 4pm. It contains advice and information about accommodation, transport, services, equipment and tour operators in Europe.

Tripsocope ☎ **020 8994 9294** can provide advice about all aspects of travel for disabled and elderly in Hungary, including help with planning journeys, equipment hire, etc.

Driving

If you are driving your own car in Hungary, take the vehicle's registration document and green card insurance with you, as well as an international driving licence. The latter plus third party insurance is required if you are hiring a car.

Detail of an apartment building on Andrássy út.

Traffic drives on the right in Hungary. Seat belts must be worn at all times in the front and outside built-up areas in the back (if fitted). Children under 12 are not allowed to travel in the front seat of a car. It is compulsory for cars to use dipped headlights outside built-up areas at all times. The most important regulation to be aware of is that drinking and driving is absolutely forbidden in Hungary; the allowed blood alcohol level is 0.0 per cent and breathalysing tests are common.

On-the-spot fines can be imposed, which must be paid in Hungarian currency and for which the police must issue a receipt. The speed limits for a car are as follows:

Motorway: 120 kph/75mph
Dual carriageway: 100 kph/62mph
Other roads: 80 kph/50mph
Built-up areas: 50 kph/31mph

There are three parking garages in Budapest, all in the inner city, plus guarded parking areas and garages as well as a number of ordinary car parks.

Electric Current

The current throughout Hungary is 220V. Plugs are the two-pin continental variety, so an adaptor is needed for UK and US appliances.

Embassies see Consulates

Emergencies

Police ☎ 107
Emergency ☎ 104
Fire ☎ 105

In cases of dire emergency, your consulate or embassy may be able to help. *See* **Consulates**

Etiquette

There are few social pitfalls to contend with in Hungary, but observing a few national courtesies will be much appreciated.

• When meeting or leaving strangers, shopkeepers etc. express a greeting rather than remain silent, which can be taken as rudeness.

• Physical contact is commonplace, and shaking hands on meeting is customary.

• Accept any hospitality that is offered with good grace and take a gift to the hostess if visiting a home.

Health

Emergency medical treatment is available free of charge from the National Health Service (OTBP), but any other treatment will have to be paid for, so full medical insurance is recommended. Local pharmacies (*gyógyszertár*) can help with minor problems. They do not sell anything except medicines and medical goods, which are mostly of East European origin. Notices in the window indicate the nearest all-night pharmacy.

Hungary is a rich source of medicinal waters and there are several baths in Budapest providing therapeutic services (*see also* p.109).

Information see Tourist Information Offices

Language

Hungarian is extremely difficult to master, being quite unlike any other European language. German is probably the most commonly spoken second language (particularly by older people), but English is gaining ground, especially in tourist areas.

As in any foreign country, an attempt at a few phrases always goes down well (*see* **Etiquette**). Note that the stress is always placed on the first syllable. To make matters worse, letters are not always pronounced the way an uninitiated visitor might think! For example, *s z* is pronounced *s*, while *c s* corresponds to the sound *ch*, and *g y* to the sound *di*. Finally, a *ü* with an umlaut is ponounced like a French *u* (otherwise it is pronounced *ou*), whereas *ö* corresponds roughly to *euh* in English...

A few useful phrases are given below.

Laundry

There are very few self-service launderettes. If you are staying in private rooms, the landlady will usually let you use the washing machine.

Lost Property

There are special offices dealing with lost property attached to all the transport services in Budapest, ☎ 322 6613 for information. Articles found in the street and other public places are forwarded to the lost property offices of the district local authorities.

If you lose your passport, report it immediately to your embassy or consulate (*see* **Consulates**).

Maps

The Michelin Road Map No

Good morning / **Jó reggelt**
Good evening / **Jó estét**
Hello/Goodbye (informal) /**Szia**
Goodbye / **Viszontlátásra**
Yes/**Igen**
No/**Nem**
Please/**Kérem**
Thank you/**Köszönöm**
How much is that?/**Mennyibe kerül?**
Where is...?/**Hol van...?**
The bill please/**Kérem a számlát**
I don't understand/**Nem értem**

Shopping in Vaci utca.

925 Hungary covers the whole country and also has area and street maps of Budapest. The *Michelin Green Guide Budapest and Hungary* includes detailed information on where to go and what to see in and around Budapest, as well as other towns and attractions in Hungary.

Michelin on the Net:
www.michelin-travel.com
Our route-planning service covers all of Europe. Options allowing you to choose a preferred route are updated three times weekly, integrating on-going road-works, etc. Descriptions include distances and travelling times between towns, selected hotels and restaurants.

Money

The Hungarian unit of currency is the *forint*, divided into 100 *fillérs* (now virtually worthless). Bank notes come in denominations of 100, 200, 500, 1 000, 5 000 and 10 000 *forints*. Coins come in 1, 2, 5, 10, 20 50 and 100 *forints*.

Money or travellers' cheques can be exchanged at banks, official exchange offices, travel agencies, tourist offices, hotels and campsites. Passports are necessary when changing money at any of these places. Keep the receipt as you will need it to change *forints* back into your own currency at the end of your stay. Do not risk changing money on the black market.

There is no restriction on the amount of foreign currency from EU countries and North America taken in or out of Hungary, but the maximum amount of Hungarian currency that can be taken out is 20 000 *forints*. *Forints* cannot be bought in the UK.

Major credit cards are accepted in hotels, department stores, tourist-oriented shops, garages and some restaurants.

Newspapers

International English-language newspapers and magazines are widely available on the news-stands and in the larger hotels later the same day. *The Guardian* and *Financial Times* arrive by midday. Local English-language newspapers include *Budapest Week* and *The Budapest Sun*, which both list events and give details of entertainment in the city.

Opening Hours

Shop opening hours vary.

Supermarkets and grocery stores (i.e., food shops) open from 7 or 8am-6 or 7pm, Monday to Friday, Saturday 8am-1 or 2pm. Other shops open from 10am-5 or 6pm, Monday to Friday, 9am-1pm on Saturdays. There is also an increasing number of 24-hour shops throughout the city.

Museums are generally closed on Mondays, and have shorter opening hours in winter than summer – some may even close down altogether (*see* pp.84-85 for details).
See also **Banks** and **Post Offices**

Police

The police (*Rendőség*) can be recognised by their blue and grey uniforms; the traffic police wear white caps. In an emergency, ☎ 107. Usually the police are friendly and helpful to tourists; few speak English, although some speak German.

Post Offices

Post offices are generally open from 8am-4pm, Monday to Friday, and 8am- noon on Saturdays. Near the Western and Eastern Railway Stations there are branches open 24 hours a day. Stamps are on sale in post offices and tobacconists.

Public Holidays

New Year's Day: 1 January
National Holiday: 15 March
  (Anniversary of 1848
  Revolution)
Easter Monday: variable
May Day: 1 May
St Stephen's and Constitution
  Day: 20 August
Anniversary of 1956 Uprising:
  23 October
Christmas Day: 25 December
Boxing Day: 26 December

Religion

The main Catholic church is
Matthias Church (I,
Szentháromság tér 3) where
there are daily services, but

One of Budapest's distinctive red mail boxes.

there are also Catholic services
at the Franciscan Church
(V, Károlyi M. u. 2; daily),
St Stephen (V, Alpári Gyula u.
5; Sun), and at University
Church (V, Eötvös Loránd,
u. 7; Sun).

Protestant services are held
at the Reformed Church (V,
Kálvin tér 7; Sun) and the
Evangelical Church (V, Deák
tér 4; Sun).

The Jewish Synagogue (V,
Dohány utca 2) has services on
Friday evenings and Saturday
mornings.

Smoking

Smoking is banned on buses,
trams and trolleybuses and in
cinemas but otherwise is widely
tolerated; *tilos a dohányzás*
means no smoking.

Taxis see Transport

Telephones

Calls can be made from public
phone boxes which require
either 10 or 20 *forint* coins or
phone cards which can be
purchased in units of 50 and
120 from tobacconists, street
vendors and some metro
stations. Telephone calls can
also be made from post offices.
When calling abroad from
Hungary, dial 00 followed by
the country code.

The dialling code for

Hungary is 36, and for Budapest 1. For long-distance calls within Hungary dial 06 first. To phone within Budapest, simply dial your correspondent's seven-digit number. For the International operator dial 09 followed by the code and number.
Country codes are as follows:
Australia: ☎ 61
Canada: ☎ 1
Ireland: ☎ 353
New Zealand: ☎ 64
UK: ☎ 44
USA: ☎ 1
Directory Information: ☎ 198

Time Difference

The time in Hungary is one hour ahead of Greenwich Mean Time, except from March to September when the clocks are put forward one hour, making the time GMT plus two hours during those months.

Tipping

Restaurants do not normally include service charge in their bills and waiters will expect a tip of 10–20 per cent. Taxi drivers also expect 10 per cent, whereas porters, guides and cloakroom attendants are used to between 50 and 100 *forints*, and gypsy violinists who play for you in restaurants expect 400-500 *forints*.

Toilets

Budapest is well served with public toilets, although those in hotels and cafés may well be cleaner. WC is *mosdó*, women is *női* and men is *férfi*.

Tourist Information Offices

TOURINFORM is the tourist information service of the Hungarian Tourist Board. English and other languages are spoken. It is open from 8am-8pm daily (October to March 8am-3pm on Saturdays and Sundays) and provides comprehensive information about tourist attractions, accommodation, places to eat and entertainment. The Hungarian travel company **IBUSZ** has numerous offices throughout Budapest, and operates an accommodation booking service and can arrange tours and excursions.
Budapest Tourist Offices
TOURINFORM, Sütő utca 2, 1 052 Budapest ☎ 317 9800
IBUSZ, Hotel Service, V, Apaci ut. 1 ☎ 118 5776
AGIP Complex, 2040 Budaőrs, ☎ 23 417 518.
Main Hall, Western Railway Station, 1062 Budapest, ☎ 302 8580.
Hungarian Tourist Offices abroad:
UK: Hungarian National Tourist Board, 46 Eaton Place,

London SW1X 8AL ☎ 020
7823 1032
US: Hungarian National
Tourism Office, 33rd Floor,
150 East 58th Street, New York,
NY 10155 ☎ 212 355 0240

The **Vista Travel Center**
(Andrassy utca 1 ☎ 309 84784)
offers both individual visitors
and groups a wide range of
services, from hotel and flight
reservations to organising
tours, car rentals, etc.

Transport

Budapest's public transport
systems consist of three metro
lines, 153 bus routes, 33 tram
routes and 15 trolleybus routes,
with four suburban train lines
(HÉV). All are cheap and
efficient and operate between
4.30am and about 11pm. Some
bus and tram routes continue
through the night. The metro
lines are colour-coded and you
have to use a new ticket each
time you change lines.

Tickets for all public
transport systems are sold at
tobacconists, metro stations
and street vendors and must be
purchased before boarding.
They are then validated at the
start of the journey (on the
vehicle in the case of bus, tram,
trolleybus and the yellow
metro line, and on entering
the station for other metro
lines) and should be retained
until the end of the journey.

The 2-day (2 800Ft) or 3-day
(3 400Ft) **Budapest Kártya** card
gives unlimited access to all
means of transport, free entry
into about 50 museums and
public places, and discounts
for some shows, restaurants etc
(*see* p.116)

All taxis in Hungary are
required by law to have yellow
number plates and be fitted
with meters that issue receipts,
but are notorious for
overcharging. They can either
be reserved or hailed in the
street. Recommended taxi
companies include:
Főtaxi ☎ 222 2222
City Taxi ☎ 211 1111
Rádiótaxi ☎ 377 7777
Buda Taxi ☎ 233 3333.

From May to September,
boat services operate from the
southern to the northern end
of the city.

TV and Radio

Radio Bridge (FM 102.1 Mhz)
broadcasts news in English
every hour from 5am-10pm
daily.

Water

Tap water is safe to drink in
Budapest but bottled mineral
water is readily available.

Youth Hostels *see*
Accommodation p.100

INDEX